Business Communication Across Borders

A Study of Language Use and Practice in European Companies

Edited by
Stephen Hagen

Languages National Training Organisation
in association with
Centre for Information on Language Teaching and Research

Acknowledgements

This study could not have been carried out without the active participation of a number of organisations in Europe, namely (in alphabetical order):

- IHK Augsburg and Schwaben

- OAVUP – L'Office audio-visuel de l'Université de Poitiers

- Salamanca Chamber of Commerce

- Spanish Chamber of Commerce, London.

Particular thanks go to Helena Christie at *InterAct International* for her careful and precise collation of the statistics from the Leonardo da Vinci-supported *Elucidate* Study. In the UK, the Department of Trade and Industry was instrumental in making recent data available from the *Language Study 1997*, which has permitted key comparisons to be made between companies in different regions. Much of the groundwork in gathering data from the West Midlands, the Northern Region (of England) and London and the South East was carried out by the University of Wolverhampton, Dudley TEC and Birmingham Business Link (Midlands); Leeds Chamber of Commerce and the North East Chamber of Commerce (Northern Region of England); and London Chamber of Commerce and LETEC in London and the South East. Finally, the entire project could not have been possible without the financial support of the Commission of the European Communities under the Leonardo da Vinci programme.

First published 1999 for the Languages National Training organisation by the Centre for Information on Language Teaching and Research, 20 Bedfordbury, Covent Garden, London, WC2N 4LB

A catalogue record for this book is available from the British Library.

ISBN 1 874016 99 2

Printed in Great Britain by Oakdale Printing Company Limited, Dorset BH17 0RS

Contents

1   *Overview of European Findings*

Stephen Hagen

The international business environment has been one of rapid change during the 90s. Companies have had to 'boldly go' to regions where they have never traded before to compete for new business against local competition.

For most small and medium-sized companies this usually means a market where the local language and local customs and business practice differ noticeably from their own. This has accelerated the process of internationalisation as companies have had increasingly to 'think global and act local'. 'Acting local' means developing strategies to overcome the linguistic and cultural obstacles posed by foreign, often distant, markets. This involves integrating new tasks, such as localising products, hiring local staff, or handling foreign enquiries, and developing the capability to operate effectively in the local language and culture.

This study compares how well companies in different parts of Europe, including Britain, are managing the language and cultural dimension in their international trade. The data used in the study are drawn from a number of sources, but primarily from the *Elucidate* project (1995-7), funded by the Leonardo da Vinci programme, and the Department of Trade and Industry's *Language Study* (1997), commissioned to benchmark UK exporters' changing communication needs as part of the National *Languages for Export* Campaign (1994-1998). A number of case studies of successful export companies are also highlighted throughout the report to exemplify instances of good practice.

Scope of the Elucidate study

The *Elucidate* survey is one of the most comprehensive research studies ever undertaken of how European business is handling the linguistic and cultural dimension of international trade. The data in the study are based on findings from a sample of 1,261 small and medium-sized enterprises (SMEs) across four European regions, namely, *Poitou-Charentes* in France; *Swabia* and the *Augsburg* region of Germany; *Salamanca* and its surrounding area in Spain and the *North of England*. The aim of the project was to identify innovative practice in the SMEs which participated in the *Elucidate* survey and disseminate examples of effective language and communication strategies to other companies in Europe.

The principal goals of *Elucidate* were to investigate:

- *levels of existing language skills*
- *spread of competence across languages*

- *levels of cultural knowledge relevant to export markets*
- *barriers to trade due to missing skills*
- *types of companies affected*
- *skill gaps/shortages*
- *impact of deficiencies on export business*
- *language training being undertaken*
- *strategies employed to overcome skill gaps and other linguistic deficiencies.*

Companies included in the samples are comparable insofar as they are

- *SMEs (with fewer than 500 employees)*
- *exporters (actual or potential).*

The findings in the study will be particularly valuable to vocational education and training organisations, including chambers, as well as the managers of international SMEs themselves. The book is also intended to inform European policy-makers about how languages are used in exporting, where the skills gaps lie, and how European companies are coping with language and cultural barriers in different parts of the world. It is divided into six chapters, including this Introduction, covering each of the regions of Europe concerned and Chapter 2 provides a short description of the sampling methods used.

For convenience, the samples are often referred to by their generic country name (e.g. the *French sample*, or *France*) even though they represent a particular region in that country. The only exception is the British sample where the survey was expanded to cover three English regions (the North of England, the West Midlands and London and the South East), thus covering a cross-section from the north to the south of the country. Data collated from these three regional samples is referred to broadly as *UK*, or *British sample*, in comparison with each of the English regional samples which are referred to by abbreviations;

NE – North of England,
WM – West Midlands
SE – London and the South East.

What language skills do Europeans possess?

Fortunately, there have been other surveys of language skills in Europe in the last few years, which give a broad picture of how different European countries compare in terms of linguistic competence. For example, in December 1996 the *Expolangues* survey of 5000 Europeans aged 15 and over found that an average of 51% of Europeans were capable of speaking at least one foreign language. The French and Italians head the league with 61% and 56% respectively. Then come the Germans with 49%, followed by the British and the Spanish with 44% and 43% respectively. In terms of 'fluency' in another language the British are bottom of the league: only 14% of respondents claimed to speak another language to a very high standard, whereas the average for Europe was 26%.

In this very 'broadbrush' picture there are three important noteworthy findings:

(i)   *Age distribution* is a significant factor: amongst the under 35s the average number of Europeans claiming to speak another language fluently rises from 26% to 37%;

(ii) *Level of competence*: The discrepancy between those claiming to be 'able to communicate' as opposed to being 'fluent' is marked. In the UK, for example, 26% consider themselves able to communicate in French, whereas only 12% declare they are 'fluent';

(iii) *English is the most widely spoken foreign language* (excluding native speakers), but not the unquestioned lingua franca in practice where a range of second languages are known: English 52%; French 39%; German 35%; Italian 26%; Spanish 23%; Portuguese 3%; Dutch 1%; and Greek 1%.

What language skills are available to European companies?

Similarly, when it comes to the industrial and commercial use of languages, it is clear that English is the most widely used language in the European regions that took part in *Elucidate*. But while English may be the predominant language in Table 1, there is also significant use of French, German, Italian and Spanish as foreign languages. Also, there is clear evidence of the growing importance of less widely used languages such as east European languages in Germany, for example, and east Asian languages, such as Chinese, in particular, and Japanese across many European regions.

Table 1: Use of languages in European companies (as % of sample)*

UK Average		Southern Germany		Central France		Western Spain	
French	59%	English	93%	English	83%	English	77%
German	53%	French	54%	German	44%	French	57%
Spanish	27%	Italian	32%	Spanish	42%	German	20%
Italian	17%	Spanish	18%	Italian	17%	Portuguese	14%
Dutch	6%	Czech	4%	Dutch	2%	Italian	13%
Japanese	6%	Russian	2%	Chinese	2%	Dutch	2%
Portuguese	5%	Croatian	2%	Portuguese	2%		
Chinese	4%						

Source: Elucidate Study
*NB figures updated late 1997

To what extent are language skills available in European companies?

The percentage of companies that have employees with foreign language skills appears to be very similar for the French, German and Spanish sample (Fig. 1 – below). The UK sample, by contrast, has the poorest language skills base with only 74% of companies declaring they have at least one employee with language skills. The exact level of the employees' knowledge is unlikely to be greater than a 'rusty O level'. This is a significant deficiency in comparison with other major European companies since the availability of language skills within the British public at large is also lower and cannot be made up easily from educational provision, particularly since the picture of post-16 take-up in British schools is poor (Moys, 1998). The key issue, however, is the extent to which this impacts negatively on trading opportunities.

Figure 1: % of companies with employees with foreign language skills

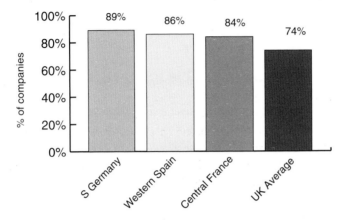

Is business being lost due to communication deficiencies?

It is clear from Fig 2. that a small, but nonetheless significant proportion of European companies have lost business due to language and/or cultural deficiencies. Spanish companies appear to be worst off (19%), followed by the British, French and German samples with 14%, 13% and 10% respectively.

Figure 2: Summary of barriers and lost business (European regions)

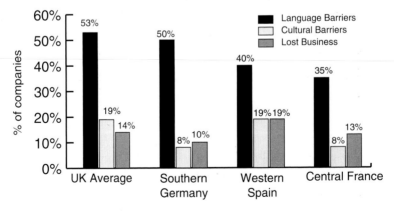

A greater proportion of companies declare they have encountered language barriers and a broadly similar percentage cultural barriers. Of these, *lost business* is the most important criterion for assessing the extent to which companies' international performance has been damaged.

For each sample, the languages causing barriers are listed in Table 3 and are virtually identical to Table 1 *Use of Languages in European Companies*. The main languages, as expected, are the major European languages where the greatest volume of trade is present. However, there has been a small, but notable increase in barriers posed by Far Eastern and Eastern European languages; e.g. Chinese and Russian respectively. There is, however, no direct correlation between trade destination and use of a particular language. The Western Spanish sample, for example, exports more goods to Portugal than any other country, yet Portuguese apparently causes few barriers to the Spanish.

Are barriers cultural, rather than linguistic?

It is clear that the linguistic interface is multifaceted, involving misunderstandings over étiquette and behaviour, as well as in the language of communication. In other words, the cultural aspects of communication are often embedded within, and inseparable from, the linguistic. In the UK sample almost one in five companies claims to have experienced cultural barriers, which is similar to Western Spain but considerably greater than Southern Germany (8%) and Central France (8%) (see Fig. 2). Many more companies face cultural barriers without realising it.

The country most likely to cause cultural barriers for French, German and British companies is Japan, followed by the Middle East (particularly for the British), Germany (notably for the French) and Italy (particularly for the Germans). Not unexpectedly, the causes are many and varied, covering a wide range of societal, behavioural and interpersonal differences. These can be culture-specific (e.g. awareness of a particular local business environment) or generic, (e.g. general lack of cultural sensitivity and empathy).

The quotations from the companies themselves show that business relationships reveal far more complex difficulties arising over differences in values, attitude and philosophy of life than from more straightforward linguistic misunderstandings.

Country	Actual quotation
China	Cultural differences are as important as an understanding of Asian or indeed other foreign languages
Far East	One needs to know etiquette/hierarchical structure/manner of conduct in meetings
France	Misunderstandings occurred through misinterpretation of cultural differences
Germany	Rigid approach to most operational procedures
Italy	"Closeness" and interrelationships within business community hard to penetrate without acceptance as an insider which can only come from cultural and social understanding
Japan	Must understand culture to do business, very significant difficulties
Mid. East	Totally different culture - time, motivation, responsibility
Russia	Inability to believe terms and conditions really are what they are stated to be
SE Asia	Strict etiquette of business in S. Korea and China, etc. can be a major problem if not understood.

A more concrete manifestation of a barrier, which combines language and culture, is the design of publicity material. This is best illustrated by a quotation from the unpublished report of a major British exporting company, which analysed local customer reaction to the German translation of its product literature.

"The trade literature needs to look 'more German' - some of the photographs are ill-chosen. This "German-ness" may be hard to define, but in terms of content it is clear that German trade literature has more technical details, such as references to standards and test methods. It can be something as nebulous as the typeface or the colour used. British trade literature can often deliberately be humorous, or use hyperbole to get a point across, whereas 'this is the biggest, boldest, best' is unsuitable to many cultures". (Quoted by German customer)

Evidence from comments in the study reveals that failure to 'culturally adapt' sales and marketing material is a major cause of cross-cultural miscommunication. Moreover companies which have successfully mastered adaptation have usually done so by adopting a 'language' or communication strategy in the first place. The above quotation illustrates the complex interplay between language, cultural expectation, visual impression and humour in written communication.

The importance of language strategies

Companies which have developed language strategies are likely to encounter fewer language barriers (see Fig. 4).

Language strategy means having in place planned mechanisms for dealing with language and cultural problems in given markets. Most companies wrongly interpret 'language strategy' as undertaking last minute language training, or bringing in translators. In fact, an integrated language strategy combines several approaches to foreseeable language barriers within a medium to long-term plan. This may involve, for example, international human resource development with multilingual document management strategies. For some companies language training, which they often consider first, may not be the best solution: it may, for example, be too expensive or progress too slowly for companies to see immediate results. For others training can be the right solution. One company, for example, used to employ local interpreters on its exhibition stands abroad until it realised their lack of product knowledge coupled with their poor understanding of the company's culture posed a serious drawback. A year later, following a programme of language training for its own carefully selected employees, the company managed not only to improve sales abroad but saved $6000 on the costs of staffing the stand locally.

Figure 4: Inter-relationship between language strategies and barriers

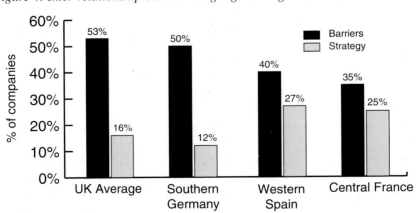

Thinking through and implementing the most appropriate communication strategy for a given company can require a far-sighted and sophisticated understanding of business language issues. Only 16% of UK companies in the *Elucidate* study, for example, claim to have formulated any kind of language strategy. Moreover, in samples of companies which face the greatest language problems, there is also less evidence of language strategies. One UK example of a company that has developed an exemplar strategy is Riley Dunn & Wilson, who were awarded the BTA *National Languages for Export* Award in 1997 (see panel):

CASE STUDY: RILEY DUNN & WILSON LTD, Falkirk. Winner of the BTA National Languages for Export Award 1997

Riley Dunn and Wilson Ltd of Falkirk and Huddersfield were established 88 years and 100 years ago respectively as expert Library Bookbinders and expert Paper Conservators and Restorers of antiquarian books, maps, parchments and manuscripts.

In order to counter the steady decline in revenue from government-funded customers the company decided to enter the export market. It undertook a preliminary export assessment by visiting French Libraries. The conclusion was that the company could compete profitably if they learned the French language and business culture and bound books to French specification.

Language strategy

- The Managing Director, his Private Secretary and the Export Development Manager started French lessons at the French Institute and later followed this by undertaking Evening Classes at three different module levels to cater for the differing levels of French.
- In addition, the Production Director, Finance Director and the Financial Accountant also subsequently embarked on French language training. The classes were carried out by a specialist French teacher who provided one-to-one tuition for 6 hours per week in the evenings on site. The company also made use of a wide selection of audio and visual French language learning material and books for self-study purposes.
- The company attended two different French Library Conferences and had their exhibition display panels translated into French. All brochures and price lists were translated into French and a French voice-over for the corporate video was recorded as a new soundtrack made available for the French market.
- The company researched the French Library Bookbinding companies and approached a small binding company as a potential agent in France. The directors of the agency spoke little English, but nonetheless, through direct communication in the language, they gained vital insights into French business procedures, legislation, culture, national heritage and protectionism, and confirmed local bookbinders' (i.e. competitors') prices, quality and turnaround.
- Riley organised an Official Press Launch at the offices of the British Council in Paris where over 100 Senior French Library figures and the Library Trade Press listened to the Director's 100 minute speech in French. This led to good trade coverage from the press launch and also subsequently received newspaper coverage.
- Lexicons of French/English technical bookbinding terms were then developed to ensure that all French customers' specifications were accurately followed by UK bindery staff. Letters and faxes were always translated; and telephone calls from the French agent and major French customers were responded to in French. All official French tenders, specification and official government communications were translated by the local professional French translator to ensure accuracy.

By understanding the French language and business culture, and exercising great patience and tenacity, the company was ultimately able to overcome the protracted bureaucratic and cultural hurdles and succeeded in obtaining the French Library bookbinding contract. One key is that the company personnel always insist on speaking French when in France as a matter of good business manners. At present, Riley's has 30 new French customers including a contract with the *Bibliothèque Nationale de France* and with *Ville de Paris*. French export turnover has risen 50-fold over a five year period as a result.

Overview of language activity in companies

In Table 4 it is apparent that, judging from the commitment to language training and recruitment strategies, there is growing awareness of the importance of language skills, if not awareness of language strategies.

Certain samples show greater proactivity in some of these aspects than others. For example, the French and Spanish samples are generally more likely to train and advertise for people with language skills than the UK and German companies. The British may do less because they hold linguistic competence in relatively low esteem (and have English), while the Germans appear to have less to do.

Table 4: Overview of language activity in companies

Company responses	Central France	Western Spain	Southern Germany	UK*
Developed a language strategy	25%	27%	12%	16%
Employees with language skills	84%	86%	89%	74%
Undertaken language training in past 3 years	31%	36%	18%	29%
Will need language training	52%	67%	38%	54%
Advertised for language skills	46%	38%	44%	25%

*Note: UK is the average of regional surveys covering North East England, West Midlands and London and the South East.

The components of a language strategy vary for different companies in different countries (see Table 5). The commonest approach appears to be to respond to communications in the customer's own language, which comes first in all samples except France. There, the tax advantages of subsidising language training make the learning of languages more affordable.

Table 5: Language strategy components

	Samples			
Strategy	**UK**	**France**	**Germany**	**Spain**
Responding in customer's language	29%	6%	24%	29%
Company and or sales lit. in foreign language	19%	-	24%	12%
Learning of foreign languages paid for	17%	68%	19%	15%
Foreign language compulsory for export sales staff	15%	5%	5%	9%
Languages are criteria for selecting staff	10%	5%	-	-
Learning of languages encouraged	5%	3%	-	-
Employment of native speakers	4%	6%	-	3%
More than 1 corporate language	4%	3%	5%	12%
All staff bilingual	4%	6%	5%	-
Use of foreign agents	3%	-	-	-
All reports in foreign language (English)	-	-	19%	18%

(as % of Companies claiming a language strategy)

Amongst all samples there are nonetheless exceptional models of good practice, where innovative language strategies have been developed and have impacted significantly on trade. These are included during the course of the book. One example of a company developing an effective strategy is Elms Marketing, which won a DTI award for penetrating the highly competitive German market for souvenir leisure ware. The language strategy involved a series of steps: selecting and sending a German speaker to research the local market in order to come up with a new set of German-style *Dungeons and Dragons* designs and emblems which fitted with local taste and culture. The planning of careful market research conducted locally in the language paid major dividends. Many companies would have been tempted to ignore the cultural dimension and ship a standard unchanged product to a foreign market with an existing design specific to their own country. In this case knowledge of both language and culture were essential to the company's success.

CASE STUDY: ELMS MARKETING, National Winner of DTI National Languages for Export Award 1996

The company identified a market for their leisurewear with different designs and emblems printed on T-shirts and tops. This needed careful research in the local market so as to understand which emblems and images were acceptable, or would be popular with local tastes, and especially with the youth culture.

The company's resulting strategy aimed to create a high level of awareness amongst staff of different ways of doing business between the UK and Germany, avoiding stereotypes and generalisations. The main elements of this strategy, listed below, combined to create overall cultural awareness and enable staff to relate to customers appropriately and service their needs efficiently.

- The company set aside a substantial travel budget to enable export staff to spend time with potential customers on the customer's territory and absorb themselves in the customer's

language and business environment, thus developing a greater understanding of their culture.
- They encouraged an on-going policy of encouraging visits to overseas trade fairs, as an exceptionally useful way of experiencing business in other countries in a concentrated form. During the first year their employees visited four trade fairs in Germany and two in France. Visits to seven fairs were planned for the following year.
- The company subscribed to various foreign trade journals and found that it was an inexpensive way of exposing staff to overseas business environments as well as providing them with language practice.
- They fostered appropriate behaviour and attitudes towards their international customers, recognising that people from other cultures have different expectations of behaviour and attitude.

Practical consequences of raising cultural awareness
- Elms changed its souvenir leisure-wear designs to Bavarian designs; German eagles as an embroidered crest, etc. which fitted with local interest and folklore.
- They developed packaging and presentation materials to increase appeal and suitability and switched to recycled materials (i.e. environmentally acceptable) and added recycling symbols to the T-shirt packaging to make it more appealing to the German market. They added their phone number with a country code so that it could be reached easily by direct dialling from abroad.
- As a result the company established a firm market share in Germany for their culturally-adapted, printed T-shirt and other leisure-wear garments.

Training – a key strategy

Critical to this process of strategy development is developing greater awareness of culture or linguistic competence by training. In recent years language learning and training have become an enormous global industry. For example, the market for English language training alone has been valued at £6 billion across 36 countries where there are an estimated 68 million students of English. By comparison, the number of students of Japanese as a foreign language is not much more than one million.

The chart in Fig. 5 shows clearly that companies in the *Elucidate* sample perceive there will be an increasing demand for language training up to the year 2000. Almost twice as many European companies plan to undertake training in the future than was the case in the past.

In the UK sample, for example, 29% of companies have undertaken language training in the previous three years compared with 47% in the 1993 *FLAIR* study. However, only half (49%) of the UK sample state that it *improved performance*. Although low, this also includes a high proportion of 'Don't knows' (28%). On the other hand, 21% (or one in five) were categorical that it didn't improve performance. Analysis of the comments indicates that this was often due to lack of commitment or lack of regular practice in using the language for day-to-day business. Lack of time was a frequent complaint: e.g. *"Classes in evening - there is insufficient time to concentrate on language training – resulting in slow progress"*.

Figure 5: Demand for language training

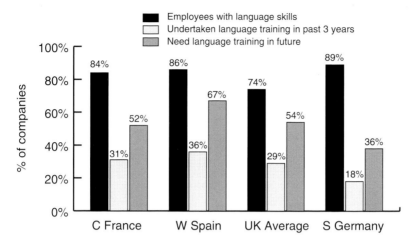

Of the companies that have already undertaken language training: 78% say they will need training in future (compared to 54% in the overall sample); which indicates that companies that have trained in the past are more likely to recognise a need to repeat in the future. Self-evidently, companies which undertake training are less likely to experience language barriers, indicating a greater awareness of language needs and a greater willingness to adopt language strategies to overcome a problem in advance.

Of the sample declaring they will need language training in the future (i.e. 54% of the UK sample):
* 80% already have employees with language skills;
* 70% have experienced language barriers;
* 43% have had language training in the past.

This confirms the general view that UK companies tend to fall into two groups: the 'language-active' and the 'language-dissmissive'. The former group already recognise the benefits, use languages in their business are therefore more likely to take action in advance by developing a strategy. The latter will continue using English for all occasions until forced to change by market conditions.

In Spain, 36% of the companies surveyed indicated that they had undertaken language training, but a higher proportion (78%) of these said it had improved their performance. Again, a higher proportion (82%) of companies that had undertaken language training in the last three years indicated they needed training in future; 62% of the companies that had undertaken training in the past stated that they did not experience language barriers, and only 38% stated that they did. This indicates a general satisfaction with training and a positive, encouraging approach in general.

The French experience was similar to the British: 31% of companies had undertaken training programmes: 58% of these indicated it had enabled them to improve their performance Furthermore,
* 52% of companies in the sample consider they will have some need for training in the course of the next three years.

- 91% of companies which forecast the need for languages already have employees
  with language skills.

Again, it is apparent that once companies start taking some measures, such as language training, their awareness of the need to develop long-term approaches also increases.

In the **German** sample, only 18% had undertaken language training in the previous three years with 60% indicating it had improved performance. Only 38% of the sample expected to require language training in the next 3 years but 63% of those who had undertaken training recently anticipated needing training in the future, again confirming the increased awareness of need following training. However, the German sample came out as being – overall – more proficient in their language capability than the others.

Translation – an industry in change

The single most important use of languages in industry is for translation. Translation is a considerable industry in terms of its size, demand and degree of globalisation. It is however undergoing rapid change with the introduction of new technologies and promises to be very different in 5 years' time. In 1989 when the last 'world survey' was carried out, the global market for translation was worth $20 billion, and growing at the rate of 20% pa. This has grown significantly during the past ten years.

The percentage of companies using translators in the *Elucidate* sample is very high across all regions:

- Germany   92%
- France   88%
- Spain   83%
- UK   83%

Translations into and out of the major European languages dominate, largely reflecting trade patterns. English is nonetheless predominant, with the volume of translations totalling between 50% and 100% greater than in the next commonest language.

Table 6: Translations by language (INTO and FROM a foreign language)

UK Average	Into	From	S. Germany	Into	From	Central France	Into	From	Western Spain	Into	From
French	32%	29%	English	45%	44%	English	47%	47%	English	47%	49%
German	27%	27%	French	29%	30%	German	25%	26%	French	28%	26%
Spanish	16%	14%	Italian	12%	12%	Spanish	16%	15%	German	14%	13%
Italian	7%	6%	Spanish	11%	11%	Italian	5%	5%	Italian	4%	4%
Japanese	5%	4%	Japanese	1%	1%	Portuguese	1%	1%	Portuguese	3%	2%
Russian	4%	3%	Czech	1%	1%	Chinese	1%	1%	Dutch	2%	2%
Scand.	2%		Russian	1%	1%	Dutch	1%	1%			
Dutch	–	2%									

(as % of total translations)

With the exception of the UK, however, companies tend to carry out most of their translation work themselves using their own employees (though this is mainly for general enquiries and correspondence) particularly for translations into the mother tongue. Use of on-line translation and Web translation services is still negligible, so the revolution promised for translation by new technology has still to dawn.

The major lever for change is the advent of telematic media, which is making the translation industry truly global. There is likely to be a split between *traditional translation* and *internet-like* business services, which enable business users to access tools and resources through the Internet; such as electronic dictionaries, machine-assisted translation devices, terminological databanks, but also give access to different levels of professional language specialists through e-mail addresses and websites. Global translation companies like Alpnet, Logos and Mendez are also beginning to develop their own intranets in order to generate translation folders, allocate jobs round the clock, provide tools (databanks, translation memory aids) to their translators, generate accounts and to create and store glossaries. Freelance translators without the technological infrastructure risk being marginalised and will require additional training in the use of the Web if they are to keep up with developments. Only the most technically adept will emerge as winners in this new global environment as the new demand is increasingly for integrated multimedia (text, sound, animation) within a multilingual documentation management system.

The need for more sophisticated multimedia effects in multilingual documentation management is partly due to a growing demand for product localisation - including software localisation - which requires highly specialist cultural knowledge, as well as linguistic expertise. Only teams based in target countries will be able to fulfil the comprehensive demands of the marketplace in future.

Additional skills required by translators now include:
- document input (scanning and OCR software)
- document retrieval
- document generation
- language information processing
- DTP and multimedia authoring.

The translations industry faces serious upheavals in its working practices over the next 5 years; firstly the increase in linguistically proficient personnel (including mobile native speakers) in many companies means more self-dependency (especially into the mother tongue); secondly, the advent of Web-based machine-assisted translation services will lead to a shift toward professional translators undertaking more post-machine editing and cultural adaptation.

Summary of key findings in the *Elucidate* European study

- Certain types of company appear to be more likely to experience language barriers. For example, size, export profile and turnover are all key variables. In terms of location, however, businesses in the UK appear to face greater linguistic deficiencies than companies elsewhere in Europe.

- English, French and German are the languages in greatest use in Europe, followed by Italian and Spanish. English clearly occupies a unique role as the predominant *lingua franca* of European business. There is also evidence of an increasing demand for skills in eastern European languages (particularly in Germany), as well as in Japanese and Chinese.

- The majority of companies in the survey indicate that they have a high proportion of employees with language skills - with the exception of the English sample - which is 12 percentage points lower than the other Euro-regions. The key interfaces requiring language usage are mainly oral/aural: *telephoning, negotiating and meetings.*

- Most international companies recognise the importance of language skills, but have not fully understood the concept of language strategies, or their value in the process of internationalisation. The need to raise awareness of how to develop language strategies within export plans is significant.

- The German and British samples indicate the highest percentage of companies experiencing language barriers. The British and Spanish samples show the highest awareness of cultural barriers; the British sample has the greatest language deficiencies and least on-site translation expertise.

- A clear subset of the companies experiencing language barriers are able to cite concrete examples of how business has been lost; more Spanish companies (19%) claim to have lost business than others. The causes vary between different samples, which suggests further qualitative work is needed.

- Companies most likely to experience language barriers:
  export less than one-third of output;
  have a turnover less than 10 million ECUs;
  have fewer than 250 employees.

- Misunderstanding local business etiquette is the single major cause of cultural barriers.

- Three of the four samples (with the exception of Southern Germany) show a clear commitment to language training, forecasting a significant increase in need. Only a minority of companies include language skills in job adverts, ranging from 25% (GB) to 46% (France).

- Language training is necessary at many levels of the newly emerging global company, particularly as a result of mergers and acquisitions (M&A activity). Regular part-time language training is the more popular form of language training except in the German sample, where intensive training is more common. Larger companies are more likely to undertake language training. There is also a need for cultural awareness training, particularly for trade in eastern cultures.

2   *Sampling Methodology*

Stephen Hagen and Helena Christie

1.   Survey aims and deliverables

The two main aims of the *Elucidate* survey were to review the foreign language needs of European businesses (with fewer than 500 employees) and to evaluate the level of existing language skills and cultural knowledge in companies. A third aim was to measure the extent to which European SMEs face language and cultural skills gaps in trade.

The principal goals were to:

- investigate levels of existing language skills of employees in enterprise;
- investigate levels of language and/or cultural training being undertaken;
- review the type of training being followed;
- measure the barriers to trade caused by lack of language/cultural skills;
- identify the languages and cultures posing the greatest barriers for SMEs;
- categorise the strategies, if any, being implemented to overcome these problems.

These findings, published in the following chapters, have enabled the European consortium to produce a series of products to assist with the development of training solutions:
- the *Elucidate* Report (i.e. this one)
- a video pack and guide in four languages versions
- an international conference (with report) to disseminate good practice and encourage networking.

A prime aim of the research was to identify companies with good practice to feature in the multilingual audio-visual training pack. The resulting video pack[1] contains 12 interviews with managers based in SMEs in France (Poitiers), Spain (Salamanca), Germany (Augsburg) and the UK (North East England) and focuses substantially on case studies where managers of different nationalities describe types of effective language training and strategies.

2.   Sampling methods

2.1   Overview

The survey comprised both a postal questionnaire and a follow-up series of telephone interviews for validation purposes. The postal survey involved mailing of a carefully designed, piloted and translated questionnaire to over 5000 companies in four European countries and was completed in mid-1997.

---

[1] *Communicating Across Business Cultures. Published by InterAct International, Ouseburn Bldg., East Quayside, Newcastle upon Tyne, NE6 1LL*

Similar criteria for selection of the companies were set for all countries: companies with up to 500 employees which are actual or potential exporters located in a definable region. In total, 1261 replies were received from companies satisfying these selection criteria.

2.2   *Regional sampling*

(i)   UK sample (UK)

The selection of companies in the NE of England sample are from the North of England region stretching from Yorkshire to Northumberland. Additional samples of companies in two other regions (London and the South East; and the West Midlands) were also surveyed to provide a cross-UK comparison. Thus, the UK results are compiled from an average of three regions giving a more general picture for the whole of the UK.

The NE samples were exporters from two main database sources - the North East Chamber of Commerce and the DTI, Leeds. The source of names for the other UK regions were from the local Chambers of Commerce, Business Links and Training and Enterprise Councils.

The mailings were carried out from May to November 1996 with up to three repeat mailshots in some regions. In the North East region 2667 companies were targeted: 160 were 'returned' due to incorrect address or 'gone away' and 83 were to companies that did not satisfy the selection criteria - either more that 500 employees or not exporters. Thus the relevant mailshot was to 2411 companies and 423 usable replies were received - a response rate of 17.54%.

(ii)   French sample (C. France)

In France, the *Elucidate* questionnaire was sent to 805 export companies in the Poitou-Charentes area and to 211 export companies in areas bordering on Poitou-Charentes; the Loire area, Centre, Limousin and Aquitaine. The overall response rate was 24% with 245 responses out of 1016 questionnaires sent out. Response was highest in Poitou-Charentes at 26.8 % (216 replies out of 805 questionnaires). For the other regions the rate was 13.8 % with 29 replies out of 211 questionnaires, which suggests the greater impact of using a 'local' base on the response rate. Although Cognac is responsible for 35% of exports from the region, the Poitou-Charentes area cannot be classified as a major exporting region (13th position among the 22 regions), although its share of exports is growing regularly.

(iii)   German sample (S. Germany)

Approximately 1.5 million people live in the district of the Chamber of Commerce for Augsburg and Swabia, which is almost identical with the county administrative division of Swabia. Around 280,000 work in industry in approximately 1,400 businesses, having more than 20 employees on the payroll; 40% of these companies are exporters. The sample of 171 export companies was derived from 830 companies in Swabia with fewer than 500 employees which were members of the Chamber (IHK). The final response rate was 20.6%, which is statistically viable for analytical purposes.

(iv)   Spanish sample (W. Spain)

The region selected for the Spanish study was Castilla-Leon, situated in central Spain where the principal industries are agriculture, automobile manufacture, other manufacturing, engineering and metal manufacturing. The response rate was 10.9% of relevant replies comprising a sample of 124 exporters out of a total target sample of 1133 export companies (with fewer than 500 employees) extracted from the Salamanca Chamber of Commerce database. This relatively low response rate is not unusual for surveys in Spain where there is a widespread concern about divulging any commercial information.

2.3 Response rate

Region	C. France	S. Germany	W. Spain	NE
Mailing	1016	830	1133	2411
Response	245	171	124	423
Response Rate	24.11%	20.6%	10.94%	17.54%

3.   Profile of companies

3.1 Central France

(i)   Number of employees

If the profile of the French *Elucidate* respondents is compared to France in general, there is a notable weighting in favour of small companies (10-49 employees).

	0-9	10-49	50-99	100-249	>250
Sample	23.3 %	41.2 %	13.1 %	14.7 %	7.8 %
Poitou-Charentes	94 %	4.9 %	0.3 %	0.3 %	0.1 %
France	92.8 %	5.9 %	0.7%	0.4%	0.2%

(ii)   Turnover

<2m ECUs	2-5m ECUs	5-10m ECUs	10-20m ECUs	>20m ECUs	No Reply
28.98 %	13.47 %	14.29 %	16.33 %	15.51 %	11.43 %

In the survey pilot it was found that some confusion had arisen over the meaning of 'KF' and 'millions of francs' which has to be taken into account. Even so, the replies tend to show that companies with a MECU 5-10 turnover are most likely to have a foreign language strategy.

(iii) Location of head office

72% of companies are fully independent, 18.78% are branches of larger French firms, 8.98 % branches of foreign firms (which corresponds almost exactly to the *FLAIR* sample of 1993), which is representative of France as a whole.

(iv) Export activity
Goods exported as percentage of total sales

0-9%	10-29%	30-49%	50-100%
37.14%	21.63%	12.24%	26.94%

37% of the companies from the sample export 0-9% of their products, and 27% export between 50% and 100% of their products. Companies' profile of export activity is not comparable with the *FLAIR* sample.

(v) Import profile
Goods imported as percentage of total purchases

0-9%	10-29%	30-49%	50-100%
68.16%	13.88%	6.12%	11.84%

The majority of companies in the sample import less than 30% of their products, and 68% of the companies less than 10%.

3.2 Southern Germany

(i) Regional profile
The breakdown of industry in the Augsburg and Swabia region is (by sector):

Steel and Automotive Industry, Data Processing	37%
Electrical Engineering	15%
Woodworking, Paper and Printing	13%
Food Industry	12%
Leather and Textiles	9%
Extracting and Processing Minerals	5%
Plastics Industry	5%
Metal	3%
Chemical Industry	1%

In 1995 industrial turnover in this region amounted to more than DM 50 billion. Approximately one third of this amount (just under DM 15 bill.) is attributable to exports.

Other EU countries account for 60% of export destinations: France is the most important export destination (12%), followed by Britain (8%) and Italy (8%). Non-European export trade is dominated by the USA with almost 8% of exports going there. The NAFTA countries produce a combined total of approximately 9% of all exports.

(ii) Sector profile

The sectoral breakdown of the *Elucidate* sample of exporting SMEs has a number of possible biases: the large number of *'other manufacturing industries'* conceals mainly businesses which do not appear anywhere else in the statistics. When measured against the regional export profile it appears that mechanical engineering is under-represented against trade and tourist industries and the construction and paper industries appear a little too dominant. The chemicals, insurance and transport fields are also slightly under-represented.

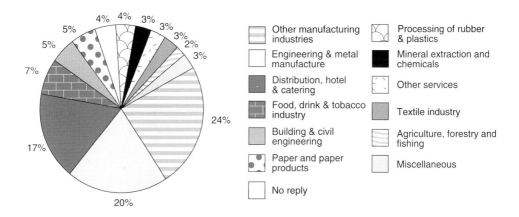

(iii) Profile by size of company, turnover and location

The distribution of employees shows a large representation of businesses with fewer than 100 employees. Companies in the 100-250 employee range are unrepresented in the *Elucidate* sample, while those in the 250-500 range are over-represented for Swabia. Smaller companies are slightly over-represented. But this may be explained by self-selection, with smaller companies more likely to experience barriers and, therefore, to reply to the questionnaire.

No of employees	%	Turnover range	%
0 -9 employees	32%	< 2 mECU	30%
10 - 49 employees	28%	2 - 5 mECU	16%
50 - 99 employees	15%	5 - 10 mECU	12%
100 - 249 employees	13%	10 - 20 mECU	10%
> 250 employees	8%	> 20 mECU	12%
No response	4%	No response	20%
Total	100%		100%

(iv)   Location of head office

Independent company	91%
Head office in Germany	4%
Head office abroad	5%

Over 90% of the respondents are independent businesses and this is in accordance with the conditions in Germany as a whole. However, the proportion of export companies could be somewhat lower. The proportion of enterprises with a foreign parent company (5%) is representative for the region.

(v)   Profile by export activity

In terms of export profile, 58% of the Elucidate sample export less than 29% of sales, which confirms that language issues are more pertinent for the small to medium-sized exporter.

Percentage of sales exported

% of sales exported	%
0 - 9% exports	30%
10 -29% exports	28%
30 -49% exports	15%
50 - 100% exports	23%
No response	4%
Total	100%

The distribution of the export share corresponds exactly to the findings of a business survey of 1200 corporate members carried out three times a year by the Chamber of Commerce for Augsburg and Swabia. However - fully appropriate for the topic - the proportion of companies exporting more than 50% of output is very high, but one must remember that the sample excludes all non-exporting companies and, thus, percentages overall will be higher.

Major export markets

Destination	% of sample exporting to country
Austria	33%
France	32%
United Kingdom	22%
Italy	22%
Switzerland	18%
USA	16%
Spain	15%
Scandinavia	12%
Netherlands	12%
Belgium	9%
Japan	7%
Central Europe	6%
Denmark	4%
Portugal	4%
Greece	4%

Given its proximity, Austria's high share may not appear so surprising, compared to the normal distribution in Bavarian Swabia, and is possibly a coincidental influence of the sample survey. It may be accounted for by the fact that smaller companies are more likely to export to nearby neighbours whereas this fact may not be obvious in analyses that include all sizes of company. Otherwise the situation described above reflects the regional picture, with the exception of the USA, which is higher than expected.

(vi) Profile by import activity

Percentage of sales imported

Sales imported	%
0 - 9%	51%
10 - 29%	20%
30 -49%	6%
50 - 100%	23%
Total	100%

3.3 *The Spanish sample: breakdown by sector, employee and export profile*

(i)   Sector Profile

The sample is an accurate reflection of the export profile of the region – with its dominance of food and drink manufacturers, on the one hand, and the manufacturing industries (including engineering), on the other.

Sector name	%
Food, drink and tobacco industry	24%
Other manufacturing industries	17%
Engineering and metal manufacture	15%
Distribution, hotel and catering	11%
Mineral extraction and chemicals	9%
Textile industry	8%
Paper and paper products	5%
Other services	5%
Building and civil engineering	2%
Transport and communication	1%
Processing of rubber and plastics	1%
Energy and water	1%
Banking, finance and insurance	1%

(ii)   Profile by size of company, turnover and location

From the tables we can see that the majority of respondents fall into the 'small' class (10-99 employees), with only 13% in the micro-class (1-9 employees). This mirrors the profile of the earlier 1993 *FLAIR* study of the Basque Region, where the breakdown was very similar.

No of employees	%
0 -9 employees	13%
10 - 49 employees	54%
50 - 99 employees	6%
100 - 249 employees	15%
> 250 employees	8%
No response	4%

In terms of turnover, most respondents fall into the < 2 m ECU category followed by those who reached a turnover of between 5 and 10 m ECUs.

Turnover range	%
< 2 mECU	34%
2 - 5 mECU	20%
5 - 10 mECU	9%
10 - 20 mECU	8%
> 20 mECU	11%
No response	18%
Total	100%

The sample is made up primarily of independent companies located in the target region.

Location of head office

Independent company	88%
Head office in Spain	4%
Head office abroad	8%
Total	100%

(iii)   Profile by export activity

As in the other samples, the majority of companies in the sample (61%) fall into the category of small exporters (40%) and moderate exporters (21%).

Percentage of sales exported

% of sales exported	%
0 - 9% exports	40%
10 - 29% exports	21%
30 - 49% exports	10%
50 - 100% exports	12%
No response	17%
Total	100%

Major export markets   (n = 124)

The pattern of export destinations demonstrate the importance of Portugal, France and Germany as the major export markets. Despite this, English is the most widely used languge of trade.

Country/Region	% of sample exporting
Portugal	34%
France	32%
Germany	29%
Italy	16%
UK	14%
USA	13%
Netherlands	9%
South America	8%
Belgium	8%
Africa	6%
Japan	5%
Argentina	5%
Switzerland	4%
Middle East	4%
SE Asia	3%

The profile of individual respondents in sample companies is also very clear-cut: 43.5% were general managers, 12.9% were Managing Directors and 7.3% Personnel Managers.

3.4 The United Kingdom sample (WM, NE, SE)

(i)   Sector

The sector breakdown used is the EC NACE classification.

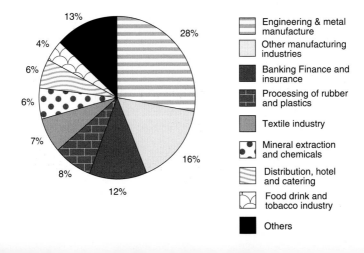

Although a very high proportion of the sample is from industry (67%), this is different from the *FLAIR* study in 1993 when manufacturing accounted for 82%. This is indicative of the general trend in the UK where traditional manufacturing industry is on the decline. However, as expected, there are regional variations: service industries in the SE sample form a greater proportion (56%), particularly in the distribution, hotel and catering sectors, whereas the proportion of manufacturing companies in the SE is much lower than for the other two regions. This difference in the profile of the different samples from each region has to be taken into account.

Sector name	NE (n=423)	WM (n=210)	SE (n=88)	Average
Manufacturing	74%	84%	42%	67%
Services	24%	15%	56%	32%
Other	1%	1%	0%	1%

In the Northern Region of England (NE), for example, the service sector represents 24% in 1996 as against only 7% in the comparable 1993 survey, which indicates a significant increase in the number of service industries in the region.

(ii)   Number of Employees

Number of employees	NE (n=423)	WM (n=210)	SE (n=88)	Average
No Response	4%	2%	5%	3.8%
0 -9 employees	17%	19%	20%	18.7%
10 - 49 employees	36%	42%	40%	39.3%
50 - 99 employees	15%	17%	12%	14.7%
100 - 249 employees	18%	14%	15%	15.7%
250-500 employees	9%	6%	8%	7.7%

The breakdown by number of employees is similar for all regions with a majority of the sample in the 10-49 employee range. Similarly, the majority of respondents (52%) have a turnover of less than 5mECU.

(iii)   Turnover

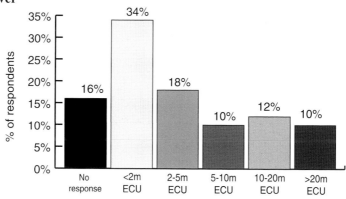

Approximately one third of respondents, the largest single grouping, fall into the 'small turnover' category of less than 2mECU.

Turnover (ECU)	NE (n=423)	WM (n=210)	SE (n=88)	Average
No Response	17%	14%	18%	16%
< 2 mECU	34%	39%	30%	34%
2 - 5 mECU	17%	19%	18%	18%
5 - 10 mECU	11%	11%	8%	10%
10 - 20 mECU	13%	11%	12%	12%
> 20 mECU	8%	6%	14%	10%
Total	100%	100%	100%	100%

(iv)   Export activity

Similar to other European samples, over 50% of the UK respondents export up to 30% of their sales.

Percentage of sales exported	NE	WM	SE	Average
No response	2%	3%	6%	3.6%
0 - 9% exports	26%	32%	25%	27.6%
10 - 29% exports	26%	30%	13%	23.1%
30 - 49% exports	14%	14%	11%	13.1%
50 - 100% exports	32%	21%	45%	32.6%
Total	100%	100%	100%	100%

(v)   Export markets for UK sample

The table below indicates the percentage of UK-based respondents in the *Elucidate* sample which export to different countries of the world. Comparing this with Table 1 in Chapter 3, the sample broadly reflects the national picture for trade with non-English speaking markets. Trade with Scandinavia is notably higher for the North East sample. If language usage follows trading patterns, the use of German, French, Scandinavian languages, followed by Far Eastern languages and Spanish might be expected. However, as is apparent in Chapter 3, trade and languages are not harmonised.

Major export markets	NE	WM	SE	Average
Germany	41%	42%	35%	39%
France	35%	33%	33%	34%
United States/Canada	33%	27%	34%	31%
Scandinavia	33%	21%	17%	24%
Far East (excl. Japan)	28%	16%	19%	21%
Spain	23%	14%	20%	19%
Middle East	18%	10%	14%	14%
Japan	14%	10%	15%	13%
Other European countries	11%	9%	20%	13%
Australia/New Zealand	14%	14%	7%	12%
Netherlands	12%	14%	8%	11%
SE Asia	11%	13%	14%	13%
Russia/Eastern Europe	10%	5%	22%	12%
Italy	9%	5%	11%	8%
Latin America	8%	2%	16%	9%
South Africa	7%	6%	1%	5%
Africa	7%	4%	0%	4%
Belgium	6%	9%	9%	8%
Ireland	5%	11%	3%	6%
India	5%	3%	2%	3%
Worldwide	4%	3%	2%	3%

3 The Communication Needs of British Companies in an International Trading Environment

Stephen Hagen

Background

International companies in Britain have become the object of more language and cultural needs analyses than in any other European country. This is due partly to the need to measure the impact of globalisation on UK exporters and partly to increasing evidence of lost trade due to language and cultural barriers. The UK is, furthermore, the only country to have set up a government-led initiative to promote the use of the customer's language in trade, the *National Languages for Export Campaign*, as a response to those needs. This chapter reviews the nature of the UK's linguistic deficiencies on the basis of findings from the *Elucidate* study, supported by the Leonardo Programme, and compares them with data from Department of Trade and Industry's *Language Studies (1995-7)* as well as the *FLAIR* (1993), and *Expolangues-Ipsos (1996)* surveys. Taken together, these studies produce a very comprehensive picture of the use of languages and cultural knowledge in UK business today.

Sources of research data

During the course of the *National Languages for Export Campaign* (1994-1998), the Department of Trade and Industry (DTI) commissioned, Metra Martech, an independent market research company to carry out annual benchmarking studies of a representative sample of circa 500 UK companies and measure exporters' need for language and cultural competence. The resulting series of *DTI Language Studies* provide the opportunity for cross-checks with *Elucidate* data. The two studies are not, however, directly compatable since *Elucidate* is only focused on England. The *Elucidate* findings are based on the weighted average of data from three sub-samples of companies (export SMEs with under 500 employees) based in the North of England (from Berwick to Leeds on the east of the Pennines) (NE), West Midlands (WM) and in London and the South East of England (SE), comprising a total sample of 721 exporters.

Changes in the international business environment

The arrival of the Single European Market and the development of global economies in the early '90s gave rise to the launch of the DTI's National Languages for Export Campaign in 1994 and the need to take action to improve UK exporters' capability to overcome language and cultural barriers. The communication difficulties facing UK exporters were exacerbated by the ongoing trend in the UK's trading pattern away from traditional English speaking markets to non-English speaking ones – a process which had developed over a thirty-year period. For example, UK exports to English speaking markets (where English is the mother tongue) have fallen to around 25% of total exports today. So the UK increasingly depends on its trade with non-English speaking counries and regions – a situation never likely to diminish from now on.

Table 1: General UK export destinations: trade in goods 1996

UK's top 10 export markets	Exports (£ mill)		Exports ranks		1996 share of UK total exports
	1995	1996	1995	1996	
Germany	20,154	20,438	1	1	12.30%
USA	18,023	19,834	2	2	11.90%
France	15,102	16,799	3	3	10.10%
Netherlands	12,256	13,237	4	4	7.90%
Irish Rep.	7,724	8,493	7	5	5.10%
Belgium/Lux.	8,295	8,458	5	6	5.10%
Italy	7,853	7,924	6	7	4.80%
Spain	6,064	6,571	8	8	3.90%
Sweden	4,113	4,385	9	9	2.60%
Japan	3,784	4,264	10	10	2.60%

Source: DTI

In Table 1 two of the UK's leading non-English speaking export markets are now Germany and France (in first and third place respectively), while the greatest potential for medium to long-term trade growth lies in areas where English has not traditionally been spoken, such as Latin America, Eastern Europe and Asia/Pacific (despite the current spate of economic difficulties). The UK's survival in this increasingly competitive and fast-moving global trading environment now involves having to learn how to develop the capability to acquire knowledge not only of the local language, but also of the different cultural norms, values and general trading practices.

The need for cross-cultural communication is, however, no longer limited to export sales teams. The flurry of cross-border activity which followed the setting up of the Single European Market has involved more British companies in take-overs, mergers, joint ventures and international links than any other European country. This process of coming together now affects many of the UK's international companies from shop floor to senior management levels, increasing the spread of languages in demand (see Fig. 1).

Which foreign languages are in widespread business use?

Figure 1: Languages in use

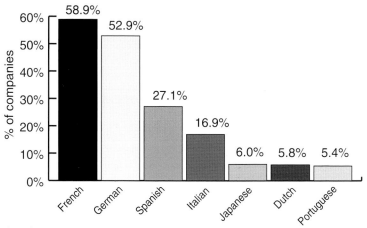

Source: Elucidate

Fig. 1 gives a broadbrush picture of which languages are used across the three English regions covered by Elucidate. Not surprisingly, French and German dominate, followed by Spanish, Italian, Dutch, Japanese and Chinese. There are noticeable regional variations. For example, the number of companies using languages in London and the South East (SE) is greater, and the range of languages more diverse, than in the West Midlands (WM) or the North of England (NE). This confirms an earlier finding of the *Languages in British Business* *('LIBB')* survey in 1988, which found that the SE sample (in that case, based in Sussex) similarly reflected a greater, more diverse use of languages skills than other regions (Hagen, 1988: xx). The number of companies with language skills has, however, grown over the years (Fig. 2.).

Figure 2: Number of languages available to companies

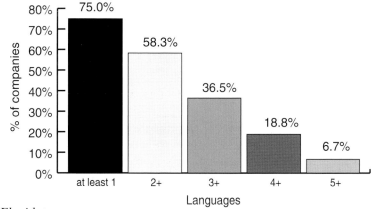

Source: Elucidate

In London and the SE, for example, over 1 in 3 of the sample use four or more languages, which is greater than in the NE (1 in 7), or in the WM (1 in 12). Furthermore, the extent to which, French and German, are used across companies, compared with Spanish and Italian, for example, is also much more significant in WM and NE than in the SE. Japanese, Chinese and particularly Portuguese, Russian and Arabic are found far more frequently around the capital and in the SE than in the other two regions. Moreover, the most esoteric languages outside the twelve commonest languages are also found in greater abundance in the SE.

A regional case study: changes in the north of England

If we examine the changes occurring in one specific region, such as the NE (Fig. 3), French and German are regularly used by exporting firms (57% and 48% respectively). These figures indicate a significant increase since *FLAIR* (1993) when the percentages for comparable sets of companies were 39% and 37% respectively. Usage of Spanish and Italian has also grown since 1993 – by 8% for Spanish (15% to 23%) and 4% for Italian (11% to 15%). Dutch has also increased in use from 4% (1993) to 6% (1996). This increase in use of languages by exporting firms is largely a result of Europeanisation, followed by internationalisation.

Figure 3: Languages in use

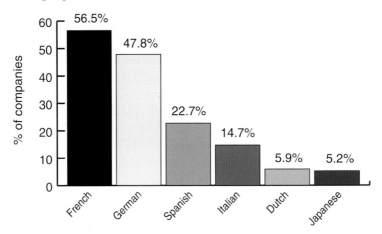

(*survey figures updated late 1997) Source: Elucidate

   One of the most interesting changes concerns the use of Japanese, which has more than doubled to 5.2%. In the *FLAIR* study 'East Asian' languages as a group was mentioned by just 3% of the sample, whereas in *Elucidate* Japanese and Chinese together are used by 8.5% of companies. Moreover, current demand for these languages in the SE is also almost twice as great as in the NE, which suggests that Chinese and Japanese have grown significantly since the 1988 LIBB study (Hagen, 1988: xx). Their usage is still small, however, by comparison with French and German, as is apparent from Fig. 4.

Figure 4: Most important languages

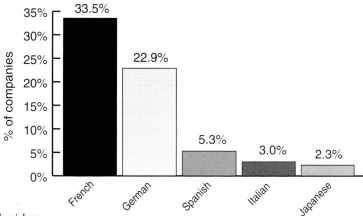

Source: Elucidate

When companies rank languages in order of importance, the differential between French and German, on the one hand, and Spanish and Italian, on the other, becomes noticeably less marked in the SE, where as many as 10% of companies declare Spanish to be *very important.*

Which specific language skills do companies need?

Table 2 indicates the use of languages by skill - *listening and speaking* dominate across all languages followed by *reading and writing* and finally *cultural competence* (which appears only to be significant in certain trading areas). Less predictably, the Table reinforces the relative importance of *reading* - only some 10% less widely used than *speaking and listening.* Nonetheless, this still suggests a slight decline in reading since the LIBB survey, which put stronger emphasis on *reading*, - which was used by an average of 58% of companies – higher than for *travelling* (53.5%) and *'phoning* (45%) (Hagen, 1988: xxv).

Table 2: Language Skills Used (Average of SE, WM, NE)

Language	Listening/ Speaking	Reading	Writing	Culture
French	54%	45%	34%	26%
German	45%	41%	29%	22%
Spanish	24%	21%	16%	13%
Italian	15%	11%	9%	7%
Portuguese	5%	3%	3%	3%
Dutch	5%	4%	3%	2%
Japanese	4%	3%	3%	6%
Russian	4%	3%	2%	3%
Chinese	3%	1%	2%	3%

Source: Elucidate

For what purposes are languages used?

The breakdown for all situations indicates that, overall, companies use languages in diverse ways; *telephoning, corresponding* and *meeting* are mentioned more frequently in Fig. 6. This reflects a change since the LIBB 1988 survey when *reading, correspondence*, and *travelling* were mentioned the most frequently.

However, the picture changes when companies rank situations where languages and cultural knowledge are used by their importance to business (Fig. 6). In this case, *telephoning, meetings* and *correspondence* dominate (30%, 25%, 15% respectively).

Figure 5: Overall frequency for each situation by % of companies (not by language or importance) (as % of occurrences)

Figure 6: Situations ranked most important for all languages (GB Av.) (as % of occurrences)

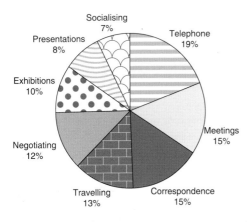

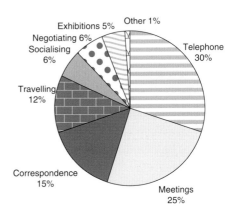

Source: Elucidate

Source: Elucidate

To what extent are companies linguistically proficient?

In the *Elucidate* Study, an average of 74% of export companies claim to have at least one employee with language skills - which correlates closely to the DTI finding of 73% in 1997. This is much greater than in the general population (see Table 7, *Expolangues-Ipsos*). This compares with some 70% of the companies in the DTI *Language Study 1996* and marks an increase over previous years of 2% p.a.: 66% in 1994 and 68% in 1995. Fortunately the picture is positive - with evidence of a growing improvement (averaging 2% p.a.) in the number of export teams claiming increased linguistic proficiency (Table 3) – though the improvement is largely limited to French and Spanish.

Table 3: European languages in which export sales team is 'proficient'

	1994	1995	1996	1997	Change (%) since 1994
French	56%	58%	60%	63%	+7%
German	50%	51%	53%	52%	+2%
Spanish	23%	25%	26%	27%	+4%
Italian	14%	15%	15%	15%	+1%

(Source: DTI Language Study 1997)

Despite the very encouraging underlying trend of increasing proficiency, there has, however, been little appreciable change in the number of companies with skills in the less common languages, where the percentage of companies with these skills is much lower:

Dutch	7%
Japanese	4%
Russian	4%
Arabic	3%
Chinese	1%

(Source: DTI Language Study 1996)

The language skills of the *home-based sales teams* have also shown only a small improvement over the last few years: 56% of the respondents in 1996 had language proficiency compared to 55% in 1995 and 52% in 1994. For the home-based staff, the contrast between small and large companies is less marked and becomes significant only for companies with more than 250 employees.

Proficiency, like language awareness and use of languages, is also closely related to company size (Table 4). The *DTI Language Study* in 1996 and 1997 indicates that the percentage of medium to large companies (> 100 employees) which had either bilingual or fluent staff is considerably higher compared to smaller companies. This difference may be linked to different linguistic demands between small and large companies. However, it could also be simply related to the fact that the possibility of having an employee with language skills is far higher in larger companies than in smaller ones. It is also clear that the smaller the company, the less likely it is to have people with any language skills at all. Also, the less widely taught a language is in formal education, the less available it is likely to be in companies.

Table 4: Claimed language proficiency: bilingual-fluent export sales staff

1997	Written			Spoken		
Employees	**French**	**German**	**Spanish**	**French**	**German**	**Spanish**
0-10	16%	9%	8%	10%	9%	8%
11-100	26%	22%	10%	26%	23%	10%
101-250	45%	35%	18%	45%	37%	19%
251-500	53%	45%	28%	55%	45%	26%
> 500	72%	53%	20%	75%	53%	30%

(Source: DTI Language Study 1997)

How well do companies cope with everyday demands?

Part of a company's apparent growing confidence at using languages is due to the availability of outside help; e.g. by contracting language problems out to professional linguists, or simply to local agents in the case of smaller companies. This trend was apparent in 1988 (Hagen, 1988: xxvi-xxvii) and the indication is that it is continuing into the late 90s. It is, however, a matter of debate whether companies should, or, indeed, are wise to, hand over responsibility for all foreign contract and communication to a third party located in the market itself.

Table 5: Company Self-Assessment of Proficiency for Given Tasks with or without External Support

1997 **Language task**	**Poor**	**Satisfactory**	**Good**	**Not applicable**
• Handling non-English speakers on switchboard	24%	32%	15%	28%
• Reading letters and faxes in a foreign language	15%	33%	30%	23%
• Negotiating contracts and agreements in a foreign language	7%	11%	26%	56%
• Preparing technical lit. in a foreign language	8%	7%	38%	57%

(Source: DTI Language Study 1997)

The apparent over-reliance of UK exporters on third parties for their language needs is due to the lack of in-house capability. When it comes to their own self-assessment of how well they cope with everyday language demands, for example, the findings in

Language Study 1997 suggests companies feel more confident about handling situations where passive skills are required; such as *reading* letters. Conversely, *handling non-English speakers on the switchboard,* which requires a more immediate knowledge of a language, has the poorest rating. This bears out the earlier, widely-known humorously unnerving studies of switchboard reaction to foreign speakers carried out by *Teleconomy* and *LinguaTel* in the early to mid-nineties, which showed that on average 75% of incoming foreign calls are abandoned at the switchboard by UK companies due to lack of comprehension.

Who uses languages in companies?

Compared with other European countries, UK export companies have less linguistic capability (75%) than those in Germany and France (89% and 84% respectively).

There are, however, regional differences across British industry. The highest figure for companies with language skills is the SE with 82%; the lowest, the WM with 67%. Figures 7 and 8 show the relative breakdown of who has these skills by company function and specific language respectively.

Figure 7: Employees with language skills analysed by job function

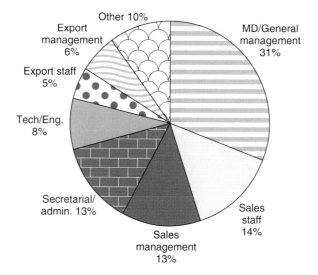

Average (as percentage of all employees with language skills)
Source: Elucidate

The majority of personnel with language skills are in *managerial positions* (31%), twice as many as for *sales staff*, sales management or secretarial/admin. This shows a trend towards *general management*, as opposed to just sales, which was also the case in the *FLAIR* Study. This is because internationalisation has led to the broadening of contact at different levels as companies have created closer alliances and started working together across the company from receptionist to shopfloor workers. This is very different to the picture in the other countries where it is secretarial and administrative staff who have more language competence (between 26% and 36%). In the UK, only 13% of employees with language skills are in *secretarial/admin.* positions. The reason for this is that bilingual secretarial training is far less well developed in the UK than in other parts of Europe. UK managers tend to possess some language skills, whereas their secretaries and administrative staff rarely do.

Figure 8: Employees with language skills relative to language

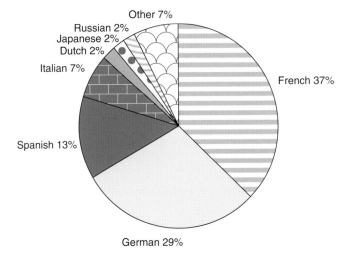

(as percentage of all employees with language skills)
Source: Elucidate

In Table 6, French remains the foreign language most available to companies. Yet while this is entirely predictable, given its emphasis in the school curriculum, what is surprising is the proportion of employees with skills in other languages, which have not been acquired at school, which particularly applies to German. It shows, however, that companies have acquired skills by some other means, either post-school training, or buying in people with existing skills, such as native speakers, which is on the increase.

Table 6: Employees with language skills relative to language (regional variations)

Language	NE	SE	WM	Average
French	38%	32%	42%	37%
German	30%	21%	37%	29%
Spanish	12%	15%	11%	13%
Italian	6%	10%	6%	7%

(as percentage of all employees with language skills)
Source: Elucidate

The number of companies in WM and NE with German, for example, is also surprisingly high compared with the SE. This is almost certainly due to the concentration of manufacturing in those regions and the importance of the German market, which has prompted companies (and their employees) into learning German. Since BMW took over Rover in the Midlands, for example, it has laid down a policy whereby all senior managers are expected to learn German by 2005, which is a good example of how global alliances can affect language needs in a 'local' company.

At first glance, the level of competence amongst employees with a language looks high. This is deceptive due to the effect of self-reporting. In Fig. 9, the largest group of employees (one-third) has only a 'Basic' knowledge of a language. There are also interesting regional variations. Employees in London and the SE are more likely to have a higher average level of competence, which is due to the employment of native speakers ('bilingual') who are more available in the London area. The percentage of employees with only Basic skills in language is also higher in the regions than in the capital: NE - 41%; WM - 38%; London & SE - 21%. This compares unfavourably with other countries of Europe, where overall skill levels are higher. It does, nonetheless, reflect figures from surveys of the population as a whole in Table 7.

Figure 9: Employees with language skills by level of competence

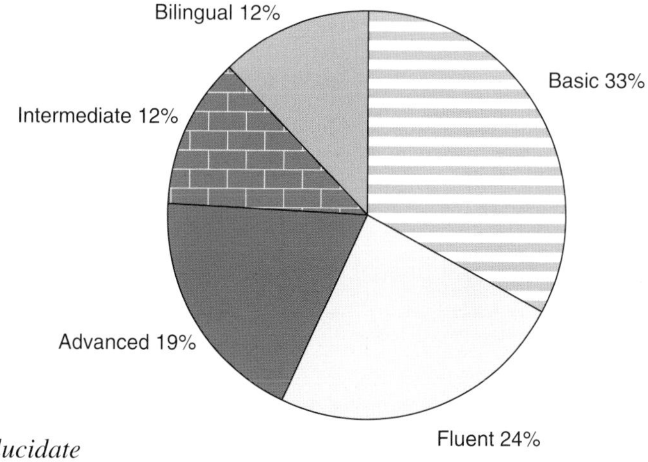

Source: Elucidate

Note: The Level of Competence, when not stated by the company, was decided on the following criteria or similar: Basic - O level/GCSE; Intermediate - up to A-level; Advanced - degree; Fluent - Masters degree or lived abroad for a long period; Bilingual - native speaker.

Language skills in the public at large

The *Expolangues-Ipsos* Survey 1996 (Table 7) gives the most up-to-date broadbrush indication of the availability of language skills in the British public at large. Based on a sample of 962 people aged 15 and over, it reveals a predictably limited range of language skills, largely in line with school provision. Across Europe the British and Spanish have the fewest number of people who speak another language with 44% and 43% respectively. In terms of *fluency in another language* the British are at the bottom of the European league: only 14% of respondents claim to speak another language *fluently* (the average for Europe is 26%).

Its findings are only approximate, however, and have to be treated with a degree of caution. For example, 36% of the sample claim they are either capable of *communicating in French* (26%) or *speaking French fluently* (10%). In practice, this probably means that 26% feel confident they can put a few sentences together and about 10% consider themselves at a standard equivalent to A level or Scottish Highers.

Table 7: Availability of language skills (n = 962)

	'Fluent'	**'Can communicate'**	**Total (%)**
French	10	26	36
German	5	12	16
Spanish	2	5	7
Italian	1	4	5
Greek	–	1	1
Portuguese	–	1	1
Dutch	1	–	1

Source: Expolangues-Ipsos Survey (1996)

What key factors influence the use of languages?

- **Do export destinations determine language usage?**

Clearly, trade destination has an obvious effect on use of languages although there is no direct proportional correlation between trading pattern and which languages a company uses. For example Germany is the most important export market for the UK. However, more companies use French than German. Similarly, Scandinavian and 'Far East' languages might be expected to be more widely used than Spanish, but in practice this is not the case.

There are of course, two principal reasons for this. The first is the widespread use of English as a primary *lingua franca* across many markets of the world, notably Scandinavia, Asia/Pacific, Middle East, Japan and the Netherlands. Also, a combination of several languages is used for communication. So a British exporter may use German in Czechoslovakia or Poland and switch to French if German fails him/her. Secondly, there is the impact of educational provision which produces four times as many schoolchildren with French than German. Companies are more likely to use a particular language if its employees have it. This particularly applies to the use of French and, to a lesser extent, Spanish. The availability of skills in German has clearly been developed beyond educational output, signifying its importance to industry and underlining an ongoing skills gap between formal educational provision and industrial need.

- **Use of English**

The existence of an *English Language barrier* for some British companies raises pertinent questions about the true value of English as the *lingua franca* of international business. Having English as a mother tongue can be a double-edged sword: it is the most widely used business language in the world (and gives British business a head start if they use it appropriately), but it also lulls English native speakers into believing that it suffices for all occasions throughout the world. One fallacy is that British English is the language of global business. In fact, between 14% (1997) and 19% (1996) of UK exporters have claimed they find British English to be a barrier to communication with foreign speakers of English. This is due to the colloquial and idiomatic use of the British variety of English, and its cultural intrusions like understatement and innuendo, which some foreigners find hard to fathom.

The communicative process is far from clear-cut anyway. In one analysis, 35% of UK exporting companies successfully claimed they used English for all transactions with their foreign customers (Metcalfe, 1991). But it has also been found that a significant proportion (16%) of business transactions are commonly held in a mixture of languages involving English in a cocktail with at least one other foreign language – not necessarily the local language. This has given rise to the phenomenon of communication as *functional multilingualism* - i.e. getting the message across in whatever language the speaker has to hand (see Hagen, 1988: 28; & 1993: 27, 28, 97).

- **Types of companies using languages (*Elucidate* study)**

On the other hand, there is a definite correlation between language usage and company type. Across all *Elucidate* samples use of languages varies according to number of employees, turnover and percentage of output exported.

In Figure 10, over 80% of companies with 50+ employees are likely to use languages. So language capability increases with size. The same is true for turnover (Fig. 11). Languages are used by 72.4% of companies with turnover of less than 5m ECU (£3.5 m.p.a.) but by 90% of companies with a turnover greater than 20m ECU (£14.3 mill.). Invariably, use of languages also increases with the percentage of turnover that a company exports (Fig. 12).

Figure 10: Language use by size of company

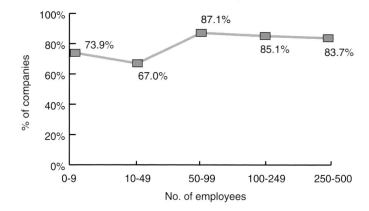

Source: Elucidate

Figure 11: Language use by turnover   *Figure 12: Language use by % exports*

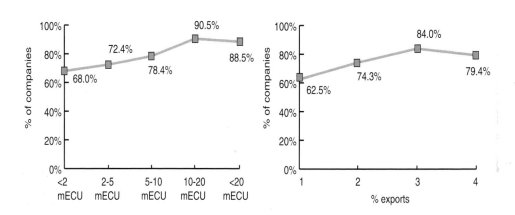

Source: Elucidate   *Source: Elucidate*

There also appears to be a somewhat surprising correlation between use of languages and age of MD: companies with MDs in their 40s and 50s are more likely to use languages, least likely with MDs over 60 and less likely for MDs under 40. The difference between the 40-50 and 60+ group is predictable and reflects generational attitudes. The difference between the 40+ and under 40s is harder to explain, but probably has to do with the age of MD being a factor in the size and growth of the company; younger MDs would tend to manage smaller companies which may not yet have the resources or export profile to make them regular users of languages. This lack of experience is also an explanation for the problems with British English above: the more seasoned exporters (with five or more years' experience) recognised English as a problem in 1996, the less experienced did not!

Table 9: Use of languages - service and manufacturing sectors

	NE	WM	SE	Average
Manufacturing/Industry	73.2%	71.0%	81.1%	75.1%
Service	64.1%	71.0%	87.8%	74.3%
Other	83.3%	66.7%	0.0%	75.0%

Source: Elucidate

Table 9 shows sectoral divergence across the three regions of England. The preponderance of SE companies using languages are in the service sector (88% service vs. 81% manufacturing). In WM they are exactly the same (71% each), whereas in the NE the majority are in the manufacturing/industrial sector, where 73% of manufacturing companies use languages but only 64% of service companies. The sector in the NE with least usage is distribution, hotel and catering (54%) whereas in the SE this has one of the highest returns. It is clear that the advance of the service sector, predominantly based in the SE, is leading to a growing use of languages in that sector than has been apparent before. This trend is likely to continue and spread from the capital outwards.

Which languages cause language barriers?

On average, over half of the companies in the *Elucidate* sample from the North, the Midlands and the SE (53%) indicated that they had *encountered language barriers in business dealings*. This appears considerably higher than the 31% in *FLAIR 1993* covering the Northern Region of England who *had missed out on trading opportunities due to cultural misunderstanding or lack of specific foreign language skills*. It is also over twice as many as the 24% of companies in the DTI UK-wide *Language Study 1997*, which recorded that 22% experienced *some barrier* and 2% a *considerable barrier* (see Table 10). It is closer to the 1988 LIBB study which found that between 60% (Yorkshire) and 25% (SE) of companies *could have significantly increased their trade performance with access to language facilities*.

These apparent differences are explicable from sampling methods and choice of question. The wording in *Elucidate* was designed to elicit more accurate information about experience of barriers. So companies were asked about the **separate impact** of *language barriers (vs cultural barriers)* and, more critically, were asked to specify whether they had lost business. The issue of *'lost business'* has been missing from previous studies. If more companies declare they have encountered a language or cultural barrier, it is important to know how many of these companies have overcome it and how many have lost business as a direct result. The DTI survey asked companies whether they felt that the lack of language had been a barrier and, if so, to what extent. Other significant variables exist in the profile of the two samples. For example, a sample which contains a preponderance of these 'high risk' features (such as small size) is more likely to experience language and cultural obstacles (see Hagen, 1993: 94, for an example of such a profile). The DTI study, by contrast, contains companies of all sizes taken from lists of users of DTI services from across all regions, which means it is likely to produce a lower percentage of companies facing barriers. It contains not only large companies with over 500 employees but also companies which, by their use of Overseas Trade Services, suggests they are not just reactive exporters and therefore more knowledgeable.

Table 10: Lack of foreign language as a barrier to exporting where English is not the first language

	1994 %	1995 %	1996 %	1997 %
Considerable	4	1	2	2
Some	21	19	21	22
Not at all	73	79	76	76

Source: DTI Language Study 1997

Figure 13: Languages causing barriers

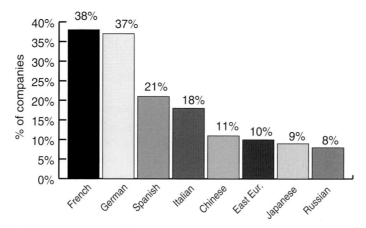

Source: Elucidate

Not surprisingly, the four main languages causing barriers across the three regions are:

- French (38%)
- German (37%)
- Spanish (21%)
- Italian (18%)

This contrasts with the findings of 1988 (covering nine UK regions). The major changes are:

- German seems to pose an increasing barrier - now almost on a par with French (and greater than French in the WM).
- Italian has noticeably risen as a barrier, almost to the same level as Spanish (and greater than Spanish in the SE).
- Chinese has overtaken Japanese as a barrier to WM and SE companies, both higher than in 1988.
- The lesser known languages causing barriers in 1988 (Dutch, Norwegian, Portuguese, Farsi) have been broadly superseded by Portuguese, East European and Scandinavian languages (Dutch and Farsi have all but disappeared, the latter due to reduced trade).

Comparing the NE sample in 1993 and in *1996*, the most significant change is the increased percentage (25%) experiencing problems with East Asian languages: 11% with Japanese, 10% Chinese and 4% Korean. This compares with only 13% of companies in the *FLAIR* survey who cited 'East Asian' languages as a barrier. This has significantly risen from 1988, when barely 7% mentioned either Japanese or Chinese. Also, Russian and Arabic have returned to pose obstacles in 1996 after they dipped in 1993 after some degree of prominence in 1988. However, since both Japan and the Middle East feature in the top ten export markets, the significance of these languages is not unexpected.

Figure 14 shows which languages are causing barriers (when ranked by importance by respondents). The order remains the same; French and German continue to cause greater barriers to a greater number of companies.

Figure 14: Languages causing barriers (1st in order of importance)

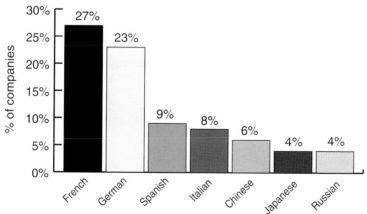

Source: Elucidate

Language barriers by key variables

It is possible to identify companies that are likely to experience language barriers by their profile. The sample of companies who had experienced language barriers was analysed against the following key variables (age of MD, sector, size and turnover) to investigate possible correlations.

Figure 15: Language barriers by age of MD

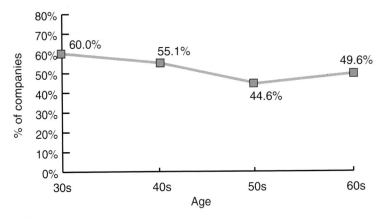

Source: Elucidate

Firstly, as in the use of languages, there is a strong correlation between age of MD and likelihood of experiencing language barriers - over 60% of companies with MDs in their 30s experienced barriers compared to 44.6% of those with MDs in their 50s. The likeliest explanations are (a) that less experienced, younger MDs are more likely to be managing smaller companies with less resource; while (b) older MDs are likely to have survived longer and developed solutions.

There are, of course, significant differences across regions and sectors. For example, 72% of textile companies in the NE experienced barriers, but only 33% did in the WM. Sectors facing barriers are:

SE: Engineering & metal manufactures; rubber & plastic processing; other manufacturing;

WM: Insurance, banking & finance; building & civil engineering; transport and communication;

NE: Textiles; building & civil engineering; distribution, hotel & catering (notably *energy and water management* - following inward investment, for example, by *Lyonnaise des Eaux* has now appeared in the list).

The average across all sectors appears in Table 11.

Table 11: Language barriers by sector

Sector name	Average
Building and civil engineering	67.5%
Engineering and metal manufacture	61.4%
Banking Finance and insurance	59.4%
Other Manufacturing Industries	58.7%
Processing of rubber and plastics	57.8%
Mineral Extraction and Chemicals	56.8%
Other services	53.6%
Textile Industry	51.9%
Distribution, hotel and catering	47.0%
Transport and communication	46.6%
Food Drink and tobacco industry	40.4%
Paper and paper products	22.2%

Source: Elucidate

Sector summary	NE	WM	SE	Average
Manufacturing/Industry	51.3%	46.6%	70.3%	56.0%
Service	44.7%	61.3%	51.0%	52.3%

Source: Elucidate

Overall across the average of the three regions, manufacturing companies are more likely to experience barriers (56%) than service companies (52%). But the difference is no longer as significant as it used to be, thus confirming the trend towards greater language use by service companies.

Figure 16 shows a strong correlation between number of employees and the tendency to experience language barriers. There is an increase in the percentage of companies experiencing barriers as size of company increases; from 52% for 0-9 employees to 63% for companies with >100 employees. Interestingly the opposite is true of French and Spanish companies with barriers decreasing as size of company increases.

Figure 16: Language barriers by size of company

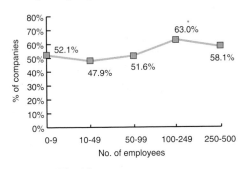

Source: Elucidate

Figure 17: Language barriers by turnover

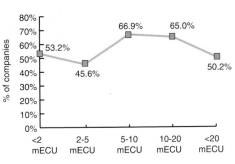

Source: Elucidate

Language barriers were experienced by only 42% of companies that export less than 10% of their sales, compared to 62% of companies that exported more than 10%.

Figure 18: Language barriers by % exports

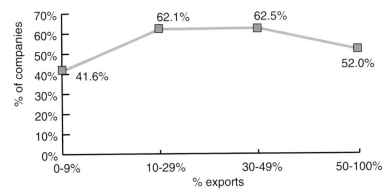

Source: Elucidate

There is clearly a peak at between 10% and 49%. Companies appear to reach a threshold at this point of exporting when language and cultural barriers become more significant.

What is the nature of cultural barriers?

Cultural barriers (see Table 12) are experienced by one in five British companies across the country (according to both the DTI surveys and *Elucidate*). Japan is the most problematic country, leading to 20% of all mentions, followed by the Middle East (14%), China and France (10%).

There is a wide range of societal, behavioural and interpersonal causes given as the reason for the barrier, some are culture-specific (e.g. awareness of local business environment), some generic (e.g. 'etiquette'). Table 13 indicates that business etiquette and management style are the most frequently cited by 46%, whereas societal behaviour (entertaining, social customs, humour etc.) is given by 12%.

*Table 12: Cultural barriers
analysed by overseas market
(average for SE, NE, WM)*

Country	%
Japan	20%
Middle East*	14%
China	10%
France	10%
Germany	7%
Far East*	7%
SE Asia[1]	6%
Italy	6%
Europe, other	5%
South Asia[2]	3%
Korea	3%
Spain	3%
Russia	3%
Other	2%
Taiwan	2%
East Europe	2%

SE Asia[1] =
Malaysia
Indonesia

South Asia[2] =
India
Pakistan
*countries not
specified

*(as % of mentions)
Source: Elucidate*

*Table 13: Causes of cultural barriers
(average for SE, NE, WM)*

Culture name	%
Bus. etiquette	35%
Social behaviour	12%
Bus/Mgmt style	11%
Meetings	11%
Time and space	8%
Honesty and truth	7%
Nationalism	5%
Negotiating	5%
Gender barriers	3%
Holidays/Religion	3%

*(as % of mentions)
Source: Elucidate*

A sample of some of the comments by UK companies explaining the nature of the cultural barrier is given below:

Country	Actual quotation
China	Long-winded discussions prior to serious negotiation
Germany	Despite the internationalisation of trade and techniques important cultural differences still remain
Italy	Long lay-offs - break delivery quotes
Japan	Etiquette problems with gifts
Japan	Initially very difficult to mix successfully with groups of Japanese businessmen - etiquette classes helped
Korea	Initial correspondence was difficult and telephone impossible. It required a visit to break the ice, since then business has blossomed
Mid East	Refuse to deal with women
Mid East	Totally different culture - time, motivation, responsibility
Russia	A dearth of cultural sensitivity and knowledge of the socio-economic status/problems
UAE	Male colleagues required to take the place of female export manager to accommodate male-oriented business environment

When analysed by key variables, the most significant factors in companies experiencing cultural obstacles is number of employees (Fig. 19) and turnover (Fig. 20). Basically, the larger the company the greater the likelihood of meeting cultural barriers. Companies with a turnover greater than 20m ECU (£14m) are twice as likely to experience cultural barriers than those with less than 2m ECU (£1.4m).

In Fig. 19 companies with 100-249 employees are more likely to experience cultural barriers, while in Fig. 20 cultural barriers noticeably grow with turnover.

Figure 19: Cultural barriers by size of company (average for SE, NE, WM)

Figure 20: Cultural barriers by turnover (average for SE, NE, WM)

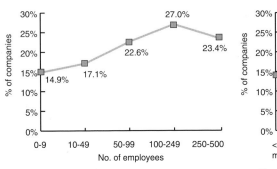

Source: Elucidate

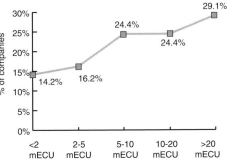

Source: Elucidate

Case study of a successful company (I)

Simpsons Photo Imaging, winner of the BBC National Language for Export Award in 1997 developed an integrated languages strategy to meet their translation and training needs which has enabled them to overcome cultural barriers and achieve significant bottom line results in Russia (see panel):

SIMPSONS PHOTO IMAGING, Stoke on Trent. Winner of the BBC National Languages for Export Award 1997

Simpsons is a company at the leading edge of the technology-enhanced dimension of the decorating industry, revolutionising the way ceramics and other hard substrates are decorated. The company's primary asset is its ability to coat hard substrates in order for them to receive dye sublimation transfers. Using this same technology it produces designer ceramic products for customers like Marks and Spencer, World Wide Life Fund, Walkers crisps, etc.

To date the company's best successes in Europe have been to modernise the way tombstone plaques (for imaging of deceased loved ones) are manufactured and decorated in Russia; assisting a mug decorator in Germany to develop and install equipment to enable him to image coated mugs and stains with dye sublimation transfers; and exporting photomugs and plates to Spain and Portugal for instant souvenir pictures at holiday resorts.

Export markets

- **Russia:** The company has customers in Moscow, St Petersburg and Ekatarinberg in the Urals. It regularly receives documents in Russian which they translate in-house. Invoices and shipping documents are written as contracts in both English and Russian. It saw a market opportunity for adapting its photomug equipment to image tombstones instead, which is now rapidly replacing the old fashioned centuries-old hand painted method of capturing pictures on tombstones.

- **Germany:** The first carefully selected advertising venture into Germany was successful. Advertising was translated into German in a colloquial manner to appeal to the German culture. The primary target is the one-man operation in any of the following markets: screenprinting, sign making, photo imaging, leisure, tourist, souvenir, gift, ceramic decorating, mail order, retail, advertising, marketing, design and promotional incentive industries.

- **Spain and Portugal:** The Portuguese distributor speaks no English and the company relies totally on an interpreter when dealing with them.

- **France:** The market has potential for decorated ceramics as well as the tombstone plaques. The Simpsons' marketing strategy includes literature, presentations, exhibitions and advertising - all in French - with aspects of French culture to be integrated.

Language strategy

- **Training/use of native speakers:** Since February 1995 Simpsons have employed a full-time linguist fluent in French and German with a working knowledge of Spanish, Dutch, Russian, Italian and Danish. He is teaching French and German to the sales staff and Russian to the Managing Director.

- The company **sends staff to train customers abroad**. To date, local staff have been trained in Russia (photomugs and tombstone imaging), Germany (dye sublimation decorating of mugs) and Hungary (photmugs). German, French, Dutch, Portuguese, Spanish, Scandinavian and Eastern Europeans visit the company for training on how to decorate photomugs, photo plates, photo tiles, tombstone plaques and other ceramic using dye sublimation technology.

- **Translation:** all letters, faxes, contracts and other documentation are translated into appropriate languages and the English catalogue has French, German, Spanish and Italian translations available.

- **All telephone calls** and meetings are conducted in the foreign customer's language. The answering machine has welcoming messages in English and German.

- **Advertising abroad:** we regularly exhibit at trade exhibitions abroad and we advertise in trade journals prior to these exhibitions. We also prepare press releases in the appropriate language and arrange editorials in European journals.

- **Cultural awareness:** our company has 16 employees and achieved a £1 million turnover last year, of which 57% was export, predominantly into Eastern and Western Europe.

Impact on business

- By the end of 1996 we had developed and sold the technology for decorating tombstone plaques in Russian and this accounted for some 8% of our turnover. By June 1997, this figure increased to 25%.

Conclusions of Case Study (I): The company believes success is due to the fact that all members of staff are trained in the cultural differences of the countries in which they do business, and are capable of clear and respectful communication with foreign clients. So far cultural awareness has proved crucial to maintaining competitiveness and remaining market leaders. Simpsons continue to pursue specific overseas markets following development of language and cultural strategies to expand export capability.

What are the causes of lost business?

One in eight (14%) of companies in the British *Elucidate* survey had lost actual business as a direct result of language and/or cultural barriers. Table 14 lists the reasons for loss of trade:

Table 14: Reasons for lost business

Reason for losing business	%
Inability to communicate (effectively)	29%
Enquiries not followed-up	9%
Can't capitalise on opportunities	8%
Misunderstandings	7%
Lack of confidence	6%
Exhibitions and trade fairs	6%
Problems with agents and distributors	6%
Lack of cultural affinity	6%
Errors in translations/interpreting	3%
Phone and switchboard	2%

(as % of companies that lost business)
Source: Elucidate

Obviously the generic *'inability to communicate'* is a catch-all, though the remainder on the list provide some insight into the nature of the language problem; agents, trade fairs and translations are clearly the major areas of communication break-down. However, actual quotations provide greater insight into company practice and approach to languages than the statistics:

"Other business had a corresponding employee who had knowledge of foreign languages so they could create better contact".

"Foreign technical experts must be trained for our equipment - this is very difficult especially for Asia".

"Interpretation of technical and legal terms cause problems"

"(Our) Reluctance to enter negotiations"

"(Our) Lack of confidence"

"Bureaucracy in F, I, Sp - easier if we had better language skills"

"Misunderstandings lead to Wrong action leads to Poor reputation which results in No Business"

"Difficult to understand customers' requirements"

"Interpreters often mistake what is said"

"Lose '(on the) spot' business at trade shows"

"Reluctance to proceed due to lack of language skills"

"(Our) Lack of languages slows progress and prevents moving forward"

"Local agents often don't have the technical knowledge"

"Misunderstanding (their) emphasis and working on wrong issues (accordingly)"

"(Our) Difficulty with on-going follow-up of mailshots/sales leads/etc."

Which companies are most likely to lose business

An analysis of companies who lost business indicates a pattern of distinguishing features. For example, 15% of manufacturing firms lost business compared with 11% of service companies. The likelihood is also greater amongst companies with 50-99 employees (an average of 18% of companies, compared with an average of 13% of companies with 99-500).

In fact, firms in the 5-20m ECU (£3.5-£14m) turnover range appear to have a greater chance of losing business through language barriers. This is similarly true for companies exporting between 10% and 29% of sales. These factors point to the existence of a critical threshold in terms of size and experience where exporters are more likely to face obstacles.

Comparisons with the DTI Language Study findings

These findings are confirmed in the DTI *Language Studies*. Certain types of company are also found to be more likely to experience language/culture barriers and potentially lose trade. Three of the determining factors from the DTI's *Language Study 1997* concur with *Elucidate* findings:

- *company size:* SMEs in the 11-100 and 101-250 employee range are less likely to have employees skilled in languages;
- *age of MD:* with MDs under 44 more likely to recognise the value of languages
- *experience of exporting:* companies experienced at exporting are more likely to recognise language and culture as a key factor.

In terms of the size of the problem:

- nearly 1 in 4 (24%) exporters recognise language as a barrier to exporting;
- 1 in 5 (19%) face (or have faced) a cultural barrier (principally in Japan, Mid-East, China, France, Germany and Italy);
- there is active language training in 15% of the companies;

- nearly 1 in 8 (14%) had found that using British English posed a communication barrier for foreign speakers of the language. Companies had apparently failed to understand the distinction between *British English* and the use of *international or mid-Atlantic* English, its abbreviated, simplified cousin;
- 94% do not recognise loss of business due to linguistic or cultural shortcomings.

The DTI findings broadly confirm those of Elucidate; the only exception is perception of the problem. Fewer export companies have faced a language barrier or claim to have lost business in the DTI Study. This is, however, partially explained by the profile of the DTI sample which contains a higher percentage of larger companies (hence, facing fewer difficulties). Furthermore, recognition of a 'barrier' is likely to be higher than recognition of lost business, since this requires evidence. What is more worrying is the *ignorance factor*, namely, the number of companies which are not aware of the impact of language deficiencies on their trade and who tend to under-report the situation. Companies are better able to report on concrete expenditure such as training.

Language training

Analysis of past language training

The *Elucidate* study showed a declining proportion of companies (29%) undertaking language training than in the previous three years (47% in 1993). This reflects the state of the economy in the intervening years. Nearly half of those taking training (49%) state that it improved performance. Although low, this also reflects the high proportion of 'Don't knows'(28%) with 21%indicating that training did not improve performance. However, analysis of the comments indicates that a number of business people felt frustrated by the timescale and lack of regular practice, leading to only a slow improvement in use of the language for day-to-day business. (see Annex 1)

Companies that have trained in the past are more likely to repeat it in the future. Also, companies which have experienced language barriers have a greater awareness of languages and are more likely to consider training as a strategy to overcome problems.

Case study of a successful company (II)

Zeneca Pharmaceuticals is an example of a company that has developed a successful in-house training programme with significant bottom-line results (see panel):

ZENECA PHARMACEUTICALS, North West England. Winner of the NatWest National Languages for Export Award 1997

Zeneca Pharmaceuticals is one of the UK's foremost exporting companies; over 93% of the ethical pharmaceuticals produced in the UK are exported and its medicines are used in over 130 countries.

The language strategy

Zeneca Pharmaceuticals recognised that the ability to work together internationally was a cornerstone of a successful global business. Many roles in the organisation involved the need to work with people in other countries (for example, consultants, government agencies, affiliated companies) and, increasingly, in teams.

A whole range of activities was developed to optimise the quality of working relationships in these areas.

Examples:

* *the inclusion of the process of international team building to examine the implications for the different cultures represented of working together*
* *advice of facilitation approaches for different cultures*
* *briefings for secondees and their families before leaving the UK and coaching for incoming secondees*
* *specific country briefings for overseas assignments and for business travellers*
* *cross-cultural communication training and briefings on specific countries for support staff*
* *language training in general.*

Language training

Zeneca Pharmaceuticals, and its predecessor ICI Pharmaceuticals, was involved in language training for over a quarter of a century but in the past five to six years it greatly increased in scope:

* Currently 28 groups, each averaging 10 participants, meet every week to study all levels of French, German, Spanish, Italian and Japanese.

* In addition, a further 25 students are receiving 1:1 or 1:2 tuition in Latin American, Spanish, Portuguese and Japanese.

* Seven secondees are currently being tutored in English as a Foreign Language.

Course content in all languages emphasises the development of oral fluency with the ultimate aim of enabling improved communication and networking between students and their overseas contacts. However, reading and writing skills are also taught.

Tutors are mainly native speakers with teaching qualifications and are employed as freelance consultants. The tutorial team meets several times a year for learning events and to exchange information and ideas.

Zeneca Pharmaceuticals is a centre for the London Chamber of Commerce & Industry's Foreign Languages in Industry & Commerce exams so those students who wish can obtain external validation of their learning. In the Summer students are entered for various levels of French, German, Spanish, Italian and Japanese.

The language programme is constantly reviewed and adapted in response to changing business needs:

Examples:

- *two groups of Beginners German were started in January 1997 at the manufacturing plant as a direct result of employees working increasingly with German suppliers and with German equipment:*

- *a new course in September "Introduction to Portuguese as a World Language", was introduced following Zeneca's acquisition of full control of a previously jointly-owned business in Brazil, more people are directly involved with Brazil; consequently the need has arisen.*

Focus on Japanese

As Zeneca Pharmaceuticals' second biggest market, Japan is vital to Zeneca. Employees from all disciplines have increasing contact with Japan. Training in Japanese language and culture started eight years ago and the Company has developed a successful strategy for Japanese:

- *"An Introduction to Japanese Language and Culture"*, consisting of thirteen 90-minute sessions, is offered two or three times a year and acts as a brief stand-alone course or as a taster for the more advanced classes. The course equips learners with survival level basic conversational Japanese built around such situations as *making introductions, greeting people, telephone communication, ordering in restaurants,* etc. In addition, it covers the structure of corporate Japan and business etiquette, generally providing an understanding of the culture and daily life in Japan.

- In the more advanced classes the reading and writing of Japanese characters is introduced. Zeneca's Japanese tutor frequently visits the company office in Osaka to familiarise herself with the different departments and to obtain authentic company-based teaching material. The company's Learning Resources Library contains a selection of videos, tapes and books to prepare people for doing business in Japan.

A major outcome of this programme is that employees feel more confident about dealing with their Japanese contacts; the effort invested has been highly appreciated and results in significant goodwill being generated.

Conclusion

As a truly global business, Zeneca Pharmaceuticals employs people around the world and welcomes diversity in its workforce. It understands the importance of respect for different cultures and the key role this can play in successful business relationships. This philosophy is exemplified in the development of language strategies, involving language training and cultural awareness training, which significantly support its export performance on a global scale.

Training by type of Course

The most popular type of training undertaken by companies is the part-time regular course preferred by 31% of companies. Less than half that number, 14%, undertook intensive training courses. The data vary across regions significantly. For example the WM figures are very similar, but the NE sample shows a preference for part-time (40%); and only 8% intensive (similar to the 1993 *FLAIR* results, 34% to 7% respectively). The SE opts for both types equally (19% each). Thus, there is a much greater use of intensive training in the SE compared with the NE region. The take-up of new technology is still low. Of 211 companies that had trained in past, 35 (17%) have used new methodology: 18 said it was effective, 7 not effective and 10 did not know. The most common technology used was CD-ROM courses. But views concerning the effectiveness of language training in general do, however, vary considerably from company to company (see comments in Annex 1).

Figure 21: Past training by language

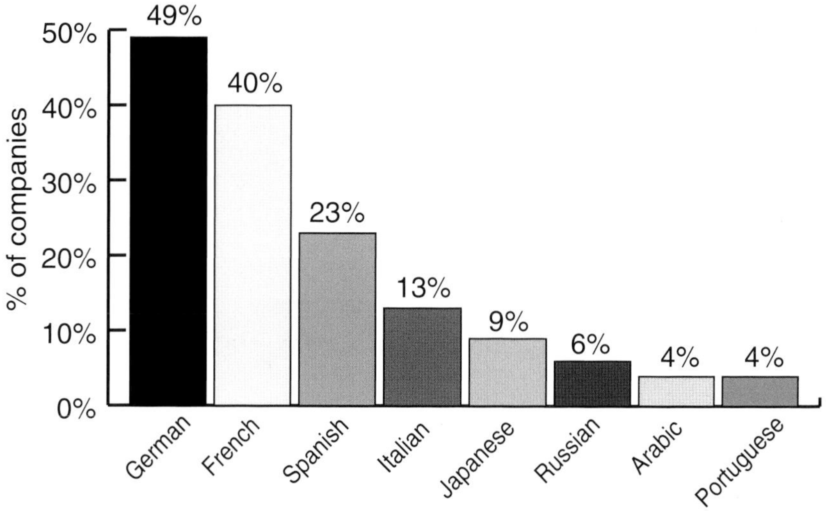

Source: Elucidate

In the UK sample of *Elucidate* and the DTI language study (1997), German is the most common language where training is required, followed by French (confirming the mismatch in educational provision). There has been a large increase since the *FLAIR* study when only 8% of the sample had trained in German compared to 14% (NE=16%) for *Elucidate*. There were also increases for French (6.5% to 12%), Spanish (2.5% to 7%) and Italian (2% to 4%), but at a lower growth rate.

Summary of past language training by company profile

• Only 18% of companies with MDs over 60 had undertaken language training compared to 24-32% for younger Managing Directors.

• Again, as for many other issues, service companies were more likely to have undertaken training in languages (33%) than manufacturing firms (26%).

- As the size of company increases so does the percentage undertaking training; for example, only 22% of companies in the 1-9 employee range undertake training, compared with 61% in the 250-500 employee range.

- A similar profile was evident against turnover.

- Companies with exports totalling 30-49% of sales are more likely to undertake training than those with less than 30% or over 50%.

Figure 22: Past Training by Language FLAIR vs ELUCIDATE

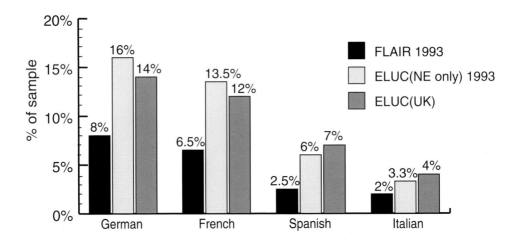

Source: Elucidate

Which languages and skills will be in demand?

Changing trading patterns

51% of the companies surveyed in *Elucidate* had plans to begin trading in new non-English speaking countries, indicating that languages would be of increasing importance. (*NB: the West Midlands sample was considerably lower than the other regions with only 43% anticipating trade with new countries.*)

It is notable that 80% of these companies had employees with language skills - slightly higher than the average of 74% for the sample as a whole. Conversely, 20% of the companies did not have employees with language skills, indicating a significant skills gap. Only 36% of these companies had had language training in the previous 3 years but 71% said they needed training in the future - indicating a great awareness of the need for language skills, but whether need is converted into action is debatable.

Figure 23: Future trading plans by country

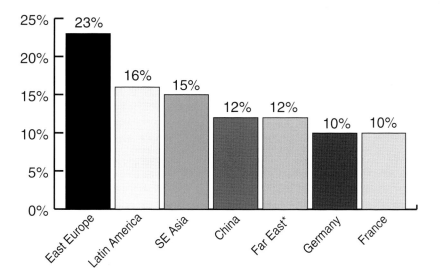

(as % of companies with future trading plans)
Source: Elucidate

When trade plans are analysed by country, 23% of the British sample anticipate trading with Eastern Europe. If Russia is included, this accounts for 32% and helps to explain the increasing importance of Russian as indicated earlier. These plans were formulated prior to the economic crisis of 1998 in Russia and are therefore in doubt. Next was Latin America (South and Central) with 16%, SE Asia with 15% and China with 12% - as Chinese is high on the list of both languages and cultures causing barriers – the need for training in Mandarin is likely to increase significantly up to and beyond 2000.

Again, there are regional differences: in the WM sample only 4% were considering Russia whereas in the NE and SE 12% listed Russia in their future trading plans. Italy, Scandinavia, Germany and France (the traditional export destinations) also featured more strongly in the WM. The NE sample also placed SE Asia much lower on the list compared to the SE and the WM.

Case study of successful company (III)

One Northern English company which expects to trade globally and has developed an effective global communication strategy is Canford Audio, winner of the 1997 NCM National Languages for Export Award (see panel).

CANFORD AUDIO, Newcastle upon Tyne.
Winner of the NCM National Languages for Export Award 1997

With its first transaction 22 years ago Canford Audio has become the largest supplier of pro-audio equipment in the UK. The business is founded upon the broadcaster sector of the pro-audio industry. In the UK its customers include the BBC, Carlton TV, Granada TV and Thames TV, as well as the vast majority of larger UK radio stations. Beyond the UK, it exports to about 80 countries world-wide; RTE, NOB, ZDF, RAI, TVE, Canal & Philips, RTBF are all regular customers.

Canford's success is based upon dealing with orders within an hour and a half with a standard delivery of 2-3 days anywhere in Europe. The holds around £3.5m of stock at any one time and has to take into account differing standards in other countries as a result of cultural and legal variables.

Canford's Export Sales dept. and Marketing dept. have speakers of French, German, Italian, Dutch, Spanish and more recently, reflecting the increasing importance of the Scandinavian markets, Danish and Swedish. It also has language capabilities in its Accounts and Technical Support departments. With around 13 foreign members of staff already, Canford has a policy of offering positions to foreign nationals, where appropriate, and has introduced a cosmopolitan culture to the company.

The language interface

- If any staff wish to increase their knowledge or level of achievement by studying for a recognised language qualification, such as the Institute of Linguists certificates, it is Canford's policy to encourage them. For the last two years, Canford has offered free courses in basic language skills to all employees through a scheme in partnership with the local authority.

- With access to foreign language skills on site, Canford, in addition to using personnel in its offices in France, Germany, Eire and Switzerland, has been able to offer freephone services. In Belgium, Spain, Netherlands, Denmark & Sweden all customers have to do is ring the relevant freephone number given clearly in the catalogue, and they will be answered by someone in their own language. These could be anything from invoices, Statements, Quotations, Credit Notes or Purchase Orders right down to the Compliments Slips and Letterheads. This is backed up by the simplicity of a local translation.

- Eleven country–specific versions of the catalogue now exist, each with portions translated to ease use for all foreign customers. Separate sections exist for Flemish & French speakers in the Belgian catalogue, German & French in the Swiss one and Gaelic and English speakers in the Irish one.

- The translation of the French catalogue involved over 800 pages and over 12,000 products – each with its own detailed description. The response to the issue of the new French catalogue was immediate. In the month since the catalogue was released there was a 19% increase in new business.

- All promotional literature is translated from English into four other major European languages, Spanish, German, French and Italian.

- Canford exhibits at around 10 major exhibitions a year. It ensures foreign language speakers are on hand to help customers, the panels on the stand are translated and brochures are available on the stands. Press Packs come in several translated versions to ease access for journalists and facilitate editorials in foreign magazines.

Since committing itself to an active exporting strategy in 1989, Canford's percentage exports against total turnover have risen from zero to 33%. In the same period, Canford became as well established in the rest of the EU as in the UK.

The MD, Hugh Morgan-Williams, feels strongly that the success is directly attributable to adopting a language strategy. For example, all personnel who interact with export customers have fluency in at least one foreign language. All advertising for staff now includes the prerequisite of a foreign language. Canford is convinced of the commercial necessity of using foreign languages - not just from the outlook of the bottom line, but on many other levels, such as goodwill and staff development.

Future demand for language training

There is a noticeable pattern of future demand for language training:

54% of the *Elucidate* sample said they would need language training during the next three years. Of these companies:

- 80% already have employees with language skills;

- 70% had experienced language barriers;

- 43% have had language training in the past.

Thus companies already using languages in their business were more likely to recognise the benefits and anticipate a future need.

Figure 24: Future training by language (GB average)

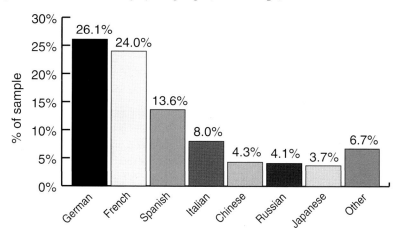

Source: Elucidate

Figure 24 shows the languages for which training is likely to be required. As usual, the same four European languages are present but German is predominant, followed by French, Spanish and Italian. The demand is similar to past training, but demand for Spanish has increased, possibly accounting for a potential increase in business with Latin American countries. Also, the percentage requiring Russian and Chinese has increased considerably from the percentage that had trained previously, also reflecting expectations of increasing trade in these regions.

Conclusions

Profile of companies facing difficulty

Given the *Elucidate* and DTI data, it is possible to develop a tendency analysis of companies likely to face language and/or cultural problems, thereby recognising the need to target particular types of company for government assistance. In both studies poor linguistic performance in companies was found to be closely linked to (i) *company size* (SMEs, firstly, in the 11-100 range and, secondly, 101-250 personnel ranges appear to face the greatest language and cultural barriers) (hence the focus on SMEs with fewer than 250 employees in the Languages for *Export Advisory Scheme (LEXAS)*); (ii) *age of company* (companies less than 5 years old face greater barriers) and (iii) age of MD; MDs under 50 are more likely to face obstacles, but are more aware of the issues. *Elucidate* adds the dimension of *turnover* (5-20m ECU) and *exports* as a percentage of total sales (10%-29%), which suggest a company can be at a stage of greater risk.

National and supranational actions

Paradoxically the UK is, by all accounts, some way ahead of most of its European partners in developing the necessary infrastructure (such as the DTI Campaign and LEXAS) required for internationalisation in its companies. This is understandable, though, given our lower starting point in linguistic capability. Fortunately, thanks to the UK taking a lead on language promotion, there is now greater recognition of the need for language strategies in other countries of Europe and a demand for more action at the European level.

The proactive stance of the UK Department of Trade on languages at a national level - and the European Commission through *Leonardo da Vinci (Lingua strand), Language Engineering* and *MLIS* Programmes at European Union level, for example, have now gone some way to addressing what is a significant national commercial deficiency. Intervention is appropriate in this case since government-led support programmes are not only intended to raise awareness of the language component within internationalisation, but also to facilitate the development of new support infrastructures at a national and supranational level to assist companies to overcome language barriers; LEXAS and NatBLIS (the National Business Language Information Service) are examples of this already happening in the UK.

In the UK changes in attitude have proved slow to achieve. However, in terms of performance there has been some progress. For example, the bench marking research in the DTI Language Studies (1994-1997) has shown a modest but notable 2% per annum increase in the number of UK companies with language skills. There has also been a more significant increase in the number of non-export teams in companies possessing staff with language skills. The number of companies claiming they have no language proficiency has fallen by 2% p.a. on average during this time. However, growth has largely been in French, while capability acquired in other languages has been disappointingly low. Hopefully, the onset of a new series of European policy initiatives on languages in the Fifth Framework, will hopefully, result in more rapid advances towards a more multilingual, internationalised workforce, not only in the UK but across the whole of Europe.

Annex 1: Comments by companies on the effectiveness of language training

Positive comments

- *Valuable 1:1 tuition for the European sales manager used weekly on phone, faxes etc.*
- *Undertaken to improve communication between local and HQ staff*
- *Undertaken mainly to understand the business and social culture better*
- *Useful to build relationships with distributors and for correspondence - it is a pleasant surprise for them*
- *Through the DTI - very good re-intro for MD and Chairman which provided springboard for current very good capability of MD*
- *Has improved possibilities to increase business*
- *More confident approach when dealing with German speaking countries*
- *More and better control of business, but always difficult to quantify*
- *Now able (with help) to make presentations in German and Italian*
- *Generates more sales and gives a competitive edge*
- *German was very good especially on phone - Germans are pleased to hear you trying.*
- *Export sales are steadily increasing. Exhibitions are more effective*
- *Improves relationship with subsidiaries*
- *Definitely able to make ourselves understood in German when normally not able to get past the receptionist*
- *Negotiated purchase of subsidiary in France with non-English speaking company*
- *Improved ability to travel but translators have been used where necessary for negotiation*
- *Gives good impression*
- *German customers respect attempts to converse in their language, even at a basic level*
- *Helps achieve profitable sales*
- *Improved correspondence and verbal skills*
- *Able to communicate more readily with export customers without having to go through export sales manager*
- *Increased confidence of staff. Understanding of 'asides' not intended for understanding*
- *Impressed suppliers and created closer understanding*
- *Customers enjoy you attempting to speak their language, it brings the client closer to you and they feel happy to deal with you*
- *Even a few words of greeting can put a customer at ease*
- *We market through Trade Exhibitions and language skills have been invaluable at European events*
- *Other languages not needed as English is the international language of our business but it helps to develop rapport*
- *Not essential - but shows willingness to converse in local language*
- *Necessary to win and maintain business*
- *Marginal value only, (but) in an International group secondment prior to in-business training is the best answer.*

- *Policy of financial support to all staff who wish to learn a language. Largely gives confidence only. Only real solution is secondment to subsidiaries abroad - we have done that too.*

Negative comments/Problems experienced

- *People offered external courses. Only works if person really wants to learn*
- *Lessons given up due to lack of time and commitment*
- *Takes a long time to become proficient*
- *German night classes - probably not hard or continuous enough to ensure fluency*
- *Classes organised at request of staff and took place after work. Only supported by a 'hard core' of interested staff*
- *Total failure - 6 weeks (1/2 day) in-house course by tutor from a university. Staff do not practise and have no confidence to try and use it*
- *All training is done in the evenings. There is insufficient time to concentrate on language training resulting in slow progress*
- *Slow progress due to time away from work required (Morning 1:1 tuition at Chamber of commerce)*
- *Little success - employees not needing on day-to-day basis were not motivated. Also frustrated by lack of progress*
- *Apart from MD everyone else dropped out*
- *On Site - good but at times restrictive*
- *No grants or incentives. No courses aimed at businessmen i.e. 8am to 9am*
- *Generally we find it quicker to employ native speakers*
- *Elementary classes - poorly attended due to travel commitments*
- *Purchased a French language CD but use quickly pushed aside by more important matters*
- *Not of great value - stopped after 2 years as not considered cost effective*
- *Basic knowledge gained but inadequate for reliable business understanding*
- *Difficult to find time to develop language skills*
- *Difficult to spend the time needed to improve*
- *Marketing Director was trained in German but has since resigned and not been replaced*
- *Dropped due to lack of relevant emphasis from teaching authority*
- *People started. 1 year later only 1 has continued*
- *Italian - unstructured course - gave up*
- *Given-up due to lack of time and commitment*
- *Because our suppliers/clients speak English our staff will not try to practise German*
- *Face to face tuition at a reasonable cost is required*
- *So many types of training that it is difficult to find the most effective for requirements*
- *Not on its own - also need quality, price etc. etc.*
- *In our experience it is always better to employ a non-English person as their familiarity with other European languages is far superior*
- *Didn't generate enough confidence*

- *Employee sent on intensive German course - left to work in Germany*
- *Work commitment did not allow the course to be completed properly*

General comments/Neutral

- *People who appear to know the language don't know it in practice*
- *English is universal language for most contracts and countries*
- *We have considered it but never implemented it*
- *Difficult to answer as trading abroad is a long term strategy*
- *Only now beginning export strategy with Germany*
- *Training commenced recently so little impact on firm's performance yet*
- *Probably not but it improves employees enjoyment of travel*
- *We recruit if possible but will train if needed*
- *Too little training to be able to assess*
- *Too early to judge*
- *Too early in the development of our business*

Comments on types of courses

- *We have an in-house language lab also*
- *The company encourages German and French to be taken at evening classes*
- *Short course aimed at business German*
- *Intensive 1:1 German course for export sales staff*
- *Used audio tapes to improve my French*
- *Intensive 1 week course for sales director*
- *Basic contact course for first line personnel*
- *Studied voluntarily by respondent*
- *Very brief reading guides prior to business trip*
- *One to one tuition/ part time*
- *For travelling abroad and living abroad*
- *In-house preliminary Japanese*
- *To give Export Manager a basic knowledge of Spanish*
- *Non vocational course due to start as part of the local TEC 'Learn for Life' initiative*
- *On-site training after work in association with local college*
- *Hours intensive course plus 2 hrs/wk ongoing*
- *Favours audio tapes in car using non productive travelling time*
- *Norwegian basic conversation as courtesy to parent company*
- *Project specific needs for Spanish and long term aim for Russian*
- *French for 18mths, 2hrs per week, 8 staff, at work. German 6 months, 4 staff*
- *Currently training in-house (weekly) for business French for Marketing and Sales managers*

4 The Language and Cultural Needs of German Exporters in Swabia and Augsburg

Nils Esmann, Dr Peter Lintner and Stephen Hagen

Background

Review of earlier research

The two most recent studies of language use in Germany focus on Baden-Württemberg (Hagen, 1993; Bruggemann, 1995). Their findings are relevant but one should take into consideration the 'small towns' bias in the former and the proximity to France in the latter.

The *Elucidate* study, on the other hand, provides a good sample of companies from Swabia and Augsburg, which is broadly representative with two minor biases which should be mentioned. Firstly, in sectoral terms mechanical engineering is under-represented while construction and paper are slightly over-represented. Secondly, in terms of the Swabian business environment, companies with 100-250 employees are under-represented in comparison with those with 250+. Full details of the profile of the sample and its degree of representativeness are given in Chapter 2.

The sample of 171 export companies was derived from 830 companies in Swabia with fewer than 500 employees which were members of IHK. The final response rate was 22.4%, which is acceptable for analytical purposes.

Which foreign languages do businesses use?

Overview of language use

In terms of frequency of use, companies in the sample fall into two clearly defined groups: (i) languages cited by at least 30% of companies in the sample (English, French and Italian - many companies cited all three); and (ii) a second lesser used grouping mentioned by fewer than 5% of the sample. English clearly heads the list of foreign languages with 93% of companies stating they have used English regularly, followed by French with 54%, Italian (32%) and Spanish (18%).

Figure 1: Languages in use   *Figure 2: Most important languages*

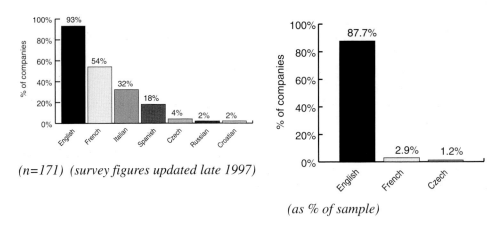

(n=171) (survey figures updated late 1997)

(as % of sample)

An overall view of the use of other foreign languages is shown in Fig. 1. The distribution of the foreign languages reflects export destinations. It is noticeable that Czech and Russian appear relatively high in the league due to increasing trade with the East.

When sampled by the language which companies considered most important (Fig. 2), a completely different picture emerges. English, with 88%, is alone at the top of the table. French (2.9%) trails by a wide margin followed by Czech (1.2%) - all other languages only reach the 1% mark or under. English is perceived as significantly more important than other languages by a very wide margin. The importance of Czech is again obvious.

Fig. 3 highlights the fact that over 93% of respondents use at least one foreign language regularly and most importantly that over one third of companies use at least three foreign languages to manage their activities abroad, which is in line with the growing diversity of export markets opening up.

Figure 3: Number of languages used

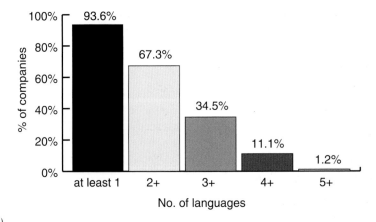

(n=171)

An analysis of the use of languages by size, sector, etc highlights a number of key features:

- 100% of subsidiary companies use languages regularly against 93% of independent companies;
- companies with over 250 people all use at least one foreign language, suggesting that size (by number of employees) is a key variable;
- usage is particularly strong (100%) in companies exporting between 30%-49% of output and with a turnover of 10-20m ECU;

This pattern suggests there is a threshold at which language usage could become critical to a company's development. That threshold is characterised by key variables of percentage share of exports (as a share of output) and annual turnover.

Language skills used

On examination of the working language skills used, it is noticeable that *listening/ speaking* takes first position in English, French and Italian, followed by *reading* or *writing*. (see Table 1). However, the sharp drop for *cultural knowledge* seems remarkable, which could indicate a major lack of awareness, a lack of skill or, conversely, a lack of need for cultural knowledge; although the latter is unlikely. The importance of '*writing* English' is due to the increasing usage of written English as a standard for corporate communication across borders.

Table 1: Language skills in use

	English	**French**	**Italian**	**Spanish**
listening/speaking	87%	48%	26%	14%
reading	82%	45%	25%	14%
writing	84%	42%	24%	13%
cultural knowledge	17%	11%	2%	2%

(as % of sample)

The skills considered *most important* are as follows:

English, listening/speaking	30%
English, writing	19%
English, reading	16%
French, listening/speaking	14%
French, reading & writing	8%
Italian, listening/speaking	8%

The emphasis on English as a world language is evident from the case of Autefa (see panel). However, it is the poor quality of their customers' English which causes barriers!

CASE STUDY: AUTEFA, MASCHINENFABRIK GmbH, Augsburg

Autefa is a German engineering company making packaging machinery. They are market leaders and trade globally; their plant can cost 10 million DM. The company is always keen to innovate and to satisfy their customers' requirements.

Their key markets are: Korea, Japan, Indonesia, Taiwan, Mexico, South America and Italy. Between 60% and 80% of their staff may be travelling abroad at any one time. Some of them can speak Spanish or Italian but there is no company pressure to learn languages other than English. In the Far East they are surprised at how poor the English spoken is. It is often so poor that they have to write down the words and use drawings.

Languages are 'extraordinarily important'. In particular, English. In all their markets it seems that 'wir kommen mit English recht gut zurecht' (we get by very well with English). Practically all of the staff learn English at school. This knowledge can then be developed in terms of a product or business by courses. But mostly their engineers develop their English on the job. In some cases their engineers speak better English than the customers.

Language strategy of Autefa

- Ensure all employees already have good English on joining company
- Supplement employees' existing English with courses and extra training at company's expense
- Identify Italian speakers in company and attach them to Italian market
- Develop knowledge of a few set phrases (politeness phrases etc.) in Korean, Chinese and Japanese (but use English for main contacts there)
- Standardise machinery to local standards and fix prices close to local competition
- Frequent visits to establish a personal relationship
- Use exhibitions to obtain local market intelligence and to make direct customer contact and feedback
- Resort to using written English and diagrams to explain issues to Far Eastern customers if their quality of spoken English is very poor.

Situations when languages are used

Unsurprisingly, Table 2 shows that languages are most commonly used whilst telephoning, followed by correspondence and negotiating. However, in Table 3, where a distinction is made according to importance, correspondence is most prominent, followed by telephoning and negotiating, while the remaining fields fall sharply.

Table 2: Situations when languages used

Telephone	22.3%
Correspondence	21.7%
Negotiatiating	19.5%
Trading	13.1%
Exhibitions	9.4%
Meetings	6.4%
Presentations	4.1%
Socialising	3.5%

(as % of total occurrences)

Table 3: Situations ranked most important

Correspondence	39.8%
Telephone	24.8%
Negotiating	20.7%
Travelling	9.5%
Exhibitions	3.4%
Meetings	1.7%

(as % of total occurrences)

Available language skills - profile of employees

Overall, 89% of the sample stated that they had employees with language skills. The difference from the percentage using languages regularly can be accounted for by nil responses to this question.

It is somewhat surprising (Fig. 4) that secretarial and administrative positions account for 26% of all employees with language skills. The unexpectedly low percentage for export staff (10%) may be due to the fact that much of the actual correspondence, follow-up and paperwork is left to administrative and secretarial staff.

The distribution of language skills amongst all employees (Fig. 5) does not reflect the local language profile of export destinations. It still indicates a high proportion of French speakers, but underlines the significance of English.

Analysis of differences in the languages and training method indicates that the highest proportion of French and English speakers are school-educated (43% and 48% respectively); this is of no surprise as it corresponds with the languages offered by the German school system.

In Fig. 6 the overall share of 20% native speakers is higher than expected and appears to follow a general trend across Western Europe towards cross-border employment to attain in-company language skills. The importance of school (38%) and part-time further education (23%) is encouraging, indicating a balanced mix of school provision and on-going training.

*Figure 4: Employees with language
skills by position*

*Figure 5: Employees with language
skills by language*

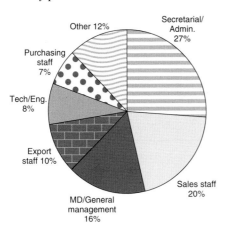

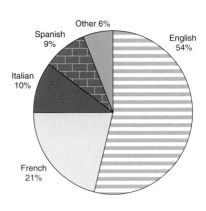

(as % of employees with language skills)

Figure 6: Employees with language skills by course

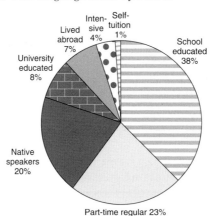

(as % of employees with language skills)

Further analysis indicates that 54% of employees with language skills report having either intermediate or an advanced level of knowledge, with 21% basic and 26% bilingual/fluent.

The distribution of competence corresponds to the frequency of usage. However, differentiation across languages indicates that there are certain language skills gaps not catered for by the educational system that have to be addressed by the companies themselves, for example, the most common means of attaining Spanish skills is by employing native speakers (40% of those with Spanish skills). Similarly, there are gaps in Czech, other East European and Far Eastern languages.

Language barriers

Overview of language barriers

A very high proportion (50%) of companies state they have encountered language barriers in their business dealings.

The rank of languages shown in Fig. 7, corresponds to the profile of the major export markets of the sample (Table 4).

Figure 7: Languages causing barriers

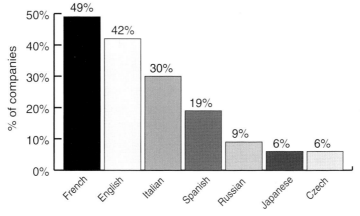

(n=86) (as % of companies with language barriers)

Table 4: Major export markets

Destination	% of Sample exporting to country
Austria	33%
France	32%
United Kingdom	22%
Italy	22%
Switzerland	18%
USA	16%
Spain	15%
Scandinavia	12%
Netherlands	12%
Belgium	9%
Japan	7%
Central Europe	6%
Denmark	4%
Portugal	4%
Greece	4%

Figure 8: Languages causing barriers (1st in order of importance)

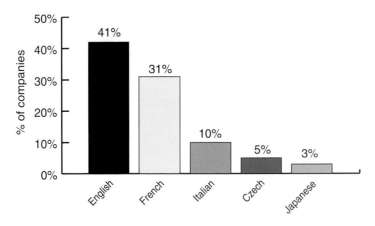

(n=86) (as % of companies with language barriers)

There are a number of apparent anomalies. Problems with French put this language first; this corresponds to the somewhat lower availability of the language in companies relative to export share. The comments in this connection are some cause for concern since they show evidence of particular obstacles in trading with France - the largest single export market in the sample. This is only slightly mitigated in Fig. 8 where English is seen as posing a quantitatively greater barrier - due largely to its greater global significance than for trade with the UK and Ireland alone. The presence of Czech and Japanese suggests that markets outside Western Europe have risen to prominence and that the local skill-base and training provision may not be adequate.

Language barriers by key variables

Distinction according to age group of MDs indicates a strong relationship between barriers and age. MDs in their 60s are more likely to experience barriers (62%) than MDs in their 30s (38%). There is little distinction between sectors, but analysis by size of company and turnover suggests that companies with 10-49 and >250 employees and those with 5-10m ECU and >20m ECU turnover are more likely to experience barriers. For the larger companies this may be explained by a possible higher volume of exports and more distant export markets. Nonetheless, it does highlight that there is a greater probability that certain types of company, i.e. in the 10-49 employee and 5-10m ECU turnover range, are more likely to experience barriers.

This is more apparent in exports as a share of output. Companies exporting between 10% and 29% of output are much more likely to have experienced barriers (63%) versus 50% for the whole sample. However, this drops significantly to only 24% of companies exporting between 30% and 49% of total sales. Our hypothesis would be that export companies are more likely to experience language barriers when exports fall into the range 10% - 30% of sales. However, it may also be accounted for by the size of companies, with larger companies more likely to export a higher proportion of total sales.

Language barriers by situations

The business situations most likely to cause barriers are shown in Fig. 9. *Negotiating, telephoning* and *correspondence* clearly account for the majority of problematic situations (67% of total occurrences). When these are analysed by individual languages the order of importance is the same with *negotiating* responsible for most barriers experienced.

Figure 9: Situations causing barriers

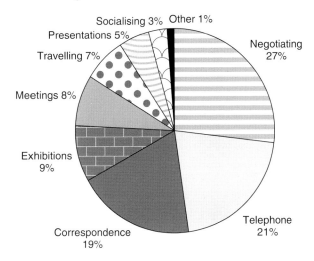

(as % of total occurrences)

Cultural problems

Only 8% of the respondents had experienced cultural barriers in their business dealings and thus cultural problems in business connections play a minor role in comparison to language problems. Of the companies experiencing cultural barriers over 38% quoted Japan as the cause with South Asian countries also well represented. The low positive response rate in this field allows few substantive conclusions to be drawn. However, the causes of barriers appear to be primarily due to differences in business practice and management style. As turnover increases, so apparently do cultural difficulties.

Gebrüder Christa GmbH is an example of a company that has a distinctive recruitment policy designed to overcome cultural barriers. It deliberately targets and recruits locally-based personnel who have studied in Germany and who appreciate the German way of doing business (see panel):

CASE STUDY: GEBRÜDER CHRISTA GmbH, Dillingen

The company produces prefabricated buildings mainly for the Third World. In most of these countries people tend to communicate either in Engl[...] either already have languages or proceed to learn t[...] have graduated from German universities, and who [...] way of working.

The company succeeds by its technological 'Vor[...] reliability and speed of response to queries. It also [...]

Strategy

- Recruits employees with existing language ski[...]
- Recruits local agents who have been educated i[...] German culture as well)
- Special attention given to learning local cultu[...] with a good knowledge of English.

Impact

Company could not conduct business without lingu[...]

Loss of business

About 10% of the sample could identify actual [...] cultural problems. It is likely that the actual p[...] peak occurs at the 10-29% export range (the sa[...] that companies at this threshold of exporting [...] languages.

Examples of how business is being lost are cle[...]

- *Competitors had a corresponding empl[...] languages and they could create contact. W[...] Russia, Japan, France, Korea, Malaysia as [...] at the initial stage.*

- *If talks in the customer's language are not [...] products. Even if the customer is intereste[...] be held and as a consequence the business [...]*

- *Communication is mainly in English at the [...]*

- *Customer-tailored orders require special [...] number of very detailed talks. The languag[...] in most cases business contacts cannot c[...] situation occurs 3-4 times a year.*

- *Orders placed rarely due to lack of English - business lost once or twice a year with France, Spain, Portugal, Italy.*

- *Communication was too difficult and business contacts have died down. We lose business to the value of 30,000 ECU approximately twice a year with France and Portugal.*

- *Translation from agency took too long as decisions in the textile industry have to be made quickly, usually on the phone. Once per year, 20000 ECU, Italy.*

- *The client would only speak French - we suspect they are isolating themselves due to language problems. We try to manage most contacts in English.*

- *Finding business contacts in F, B, UK via third parties (agencies, consultants, etc.) is too difficult. Any contacts we have come about by accident. We lose business approximately three times per year totalling 50,000 ECU.*

- *Business contacts die during initial discussions due to language problems and difficult financial conditions. Deals are usually done by phone requiring quick decisions. We lose business 2-3 times/year, to the value of 5000 ECU with France.*

- *With Spain we need to speak Spanish - most contacts have died down due to the langi ~~ barrier We lose business 4-5 times/year, totalling 50000 ECU to Spain.*

- *Com   ne in English but usually*
  there   want to be addressed in
  Fren   guage problems prevented
  us fi

- *Inqi   could not follow-up with*
  tele   ess 2-3 times/year, France,
  Hui

Com

The p   171) who have developed
foreig   ts there is major scope for
initiat   When compared to other
sampl   Central France and Western
Spain   ctively, and there is a very
stron   : strategy and avoidance of
langu

Fc   nies with a language strategy
had   en training in the past (43%)
than   :ly). One interesting example
of th   hich takes a team approach to
thei   ction of personnel has created
a hi   inel):

CASE STUDY: BTG MESSE-SPEDITION GmbH, Augsburg

BTG Messe-Spedition specialises in trade fair haulage on a world-wide basis. They deal with many different nationalities and so their employees must have good English plus at least one other language to begin with. They work and train in teams and when they attend trade fairs they target specific languages, and learn Spanish and Russian, in 'Arbeitsgruppen' (study groups) with a teacher brought in. Although working in teams they are very flexible and depend upon individuals to be co-operative and to keep themselves up to date, or even to decide for themselves which new language they feel they need to acquire (currently Chinese). They do not employ introverts; colleagues have to be good with people, friendly, with a sense of humour, as well as competent in the business and attentive to detail. The MD is convinced that you do business better if you can use the customer's language and can understand the culture, which includes 'gepflegte Umgangsformen', polished manners. In China for example, they had to use gestures and body language due to their lack of Chinese.

Strategy

- Select employees for suitable personality traits, manners and team-work; i.e. profiling of 'internationally sensitive' individuals.

- Employees must have English, plus one other language, before they are selected

- Create market-focused teams who speak local language

- Trainers brought in to tutor whole team in local language, particularly for specialised expressions

When analysing the use of foreign language training, 18% of companies had undertaken language training in the previous three year. This is considerably lower than for the other three samples (from 29 - 36%) and may be explained by the fact that only 12% of the German sample had developed a language strategy. 60% of the companies that had undertaken language training stated that it had improved performance, with 17% quoting no improvement and 23% unsure.

Of the companies that had taken training courses, 63% intend to train again in the future. Although this appears low it is significantly higher than the percentage of the whole sample planning language training in the future (38%) and thus confirms the hypothesis that companies who undertake language training are more likely to repeat it. There is also a slight correlation between experience with language barriers and training carried out in the past with only 43% of these companies experiencing language barriers compared to 50% for the sample as a whole.

There is a very strong correlation between turnover and language training as shown in Fig. 10 – where 45% of companies with turnover in excess of 20m ECU had undertaken language training against only 4% of those with less than 2m ECU.

Figure 10: Past Training by turnover

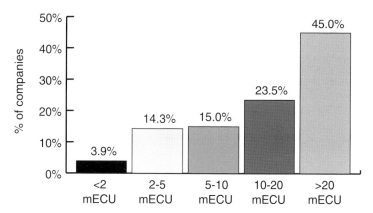

Obviously, little use is found for new methods in teaching language (PC, CD-ROM) as only 3% use these methods, however, all these companies found these new methods very effective.

It was not unexpected to find past language courses mainly at larger companies with 100 or more employees - 39% of companies with 100-249 employees against only 11% of those with less than 50 employees. These courses have become more important in industry, especially for the field of engineering and metal manufacture (27%), a fact which can be explained by its high export quota.

There was also a major difference between companies based on ownership with 44% of subsidiaries having followed training against only 15% of independent companies.

Of the companies sampled, 92% require translations. These are most commonly done by employees (63% of all translations carried out into a foreign language and 72% into German) but professional translators are also used widely, with 24% of translations from a foreign language into German and 31% from German into the target language. The most common languages for which translations are required are English (45% of all translations); French 29%; Italian 12% and Spanish 11%. The types of documents requiring translation are predominantly correspondence and enquiries which account for 43% of all translations, followed by sales literature (10% of translations into a foreign language) and technical (6% from German).

Future demand for foreign languages

Nearly two thirds of enterprises are trying to open up new markets for their export activities; possibly, the impact of the EU plays a very special role here. Nearly one third of the businesses pointed out that they have greater confidence into expanding in the more familiar European (EU) markets, however, Eastern Europe, the Far East and South East Asia also figure prominently as target markets.

Of the companies with future trading plans in new non-German speaking countries, 94% already have in-house language skills, 21% have undertaken training in the past three years and, most significantly, 47% recognise they will need training in the next three years. Of all companies in the survey, over one third of the companies interviewed (38%) will require language training, with more than half (55%) answering in the negative. Top of the list of required languages for almost one third of the companies interviewed (29%) is English (77% of companies needing training), but also French (15%), indicating a continuing high demand. The unexpectedly high level of demand for Italian and Spanish (9% and 6% of businesses respectively) shows an increase which could meet a shortage of provision since in the past training in these languages was carried out by only 2% and 1% of businesses.

It is interesting that 91% of employees from companies which need training in foreign languages already have some linguistic knowledge, which is obviously seen as inadequate. Also, the relatively high number (69%) of companies considering training that have experienced barriers in the past indicates that their skills gap in foreign languages is likely to pose a barrier in future.

This is also borne out of by data from the Expolangues-Ipsos survey (1996:15) which indicates that linguistic competence amongst the general population of Germany is limited mainly to English. For example, 25% of Germans declare themselves 'fluent' in English and 22% 'competent', while only 4% indicate they are 'fluent' in French and 8% 'competent'. Competence in other languages is highly limited with fewer than 3% claiming any competence in Spanish, Italian or Dutch. Skills in other languages are negligible.

Conclusions

The most obvious conclusion arising from the study is that German companies are likely to meet skill shortages in languages other than English as trade expands in both Europe (particularly eastwards) and the rest of the world (particularly the Far East, S E Asia and Latin America).

German companies do have a significant take-up of training opportunities and a balanced mix of using skills acquired at school, at evening class and gained by the employment of native speakers (20%). The lack of recognition of the importance of cultural awareness is disconcerting.

Particular types of company risk facing language and cultural barriers. These can be identified from key variables. For example, companies exporting between 10% and 29% of output; those with older MDs (over 60); companies with 10-49 or 250-500 employees and those with 5-10 m ECU or >20 m ECU in turnover demonstrate a greater tendency to experience barriers. This suggests there is a pattern of need that could, and should, be addressed by government or EU intervention.

5 Foreign Language Use and The Needs of Spanish Exporters in Central Spain

Nasreen Ali, Manuel José García Vicente, José Fernandez Bragado and Stephen Hagen

Background

Few studies exist of language usage by Spanish exporters. The primary reasons for this are the lack of a strong and active research base in industry-focused applied languages studies in Spanish universities and the natural diffidence of owner-managers about releasing commercially sensitive information. Prior to this study, the most comprehensive was the *FLAIR* survey (Castro Calvin, 1993) which focused on 348 export companies in the Basque Region. The *Expolangues-Ipsos Europe* poll also gives an approximate picture of language skills amongst the population at large. *Elucidate*, which focused on Castilla-Leon, provides an important additional piece of the jigsaw with a profile of language activities in 124 export companies sampled from the Salamanca Chamber of Commerce database[1]

Which languages are used?

English is the most frequently used language in the *Elucidate* sample with 77%, (Fig. 1) closely followed by French with 57%, German with 20%, Portuguese (14%) and Italian (13%).

Figure 1: Languages in use

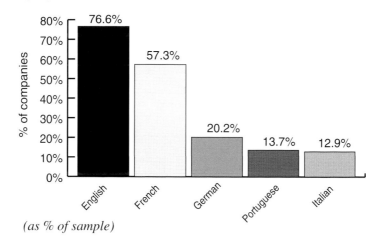

(n=124)   (as % of sample)

This order not unexpectedly corresponds to the *Expolangue-Ipsos* survey with the exception of German, where usage is much more pronounced in *Elucidate* than in *Expolangues* (Fig. 2).

Figure 2: European Languages spoken by Spanish people

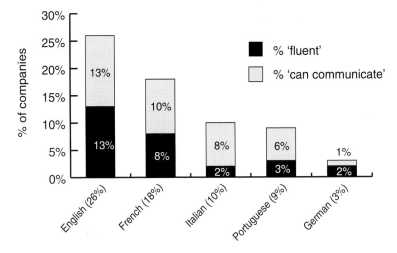

(n=690 individuals (of 15+ years))
Source: Expolangues-Ipsos Europe (1996) p14

Compared with the *FLAIR* findings, use of English in *Elucidate* appears to be far more widespread (77% *Elucidate* and 49% *FLAIR*). German is of a similar proportion with slightly higher use (15% in *FLAIR* and 20% in *Elucidate*). French is high in both, having comparatively risen from 44% to 57%. The samples are not strictly comparable, but it is worth making the hypothesis that use of languages appears to have increased in the nineties with English and German coming to greater prominence. The increasing importance of German has been noted elsewhere (Castro Calvin, ibid; P45).

Most important languages

The predominant position of English is even more apparent when companies indicate which language was the most important to their business activity: nearly 57% quote English, followed by French (16%). Other languages fall below 4% of the sample (Fig. 3).

Almost 83% of companies use at least one language on a regular working basis and nearly two-thirds use two languages; 26% use three, 11% use four and 5% use five or more (Fig. 4). This is broadly comparable to the data from French companies and proportionally greater than in the British sample.

Figure 3: Most important languages

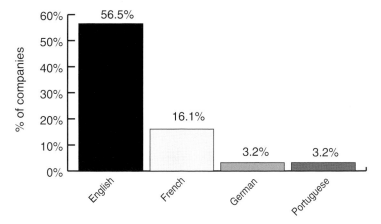

(n=124) (as % of sample)

Figure 4: Number of languages used

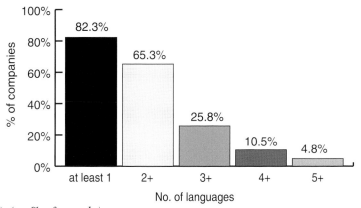

(n=124) (as % of sample)

Is the use of languages directly related to export destinations?

Use of languages does not directly correlate with the native languages spoken in the export markets. For example, Portugal is the major market for companies in the sample (34%), followed by France (32%), Germany (29%), Italy (16%), UK (14%), the United States (13%), Netherlands (9%).

Portugal is the number one export market, but Portuguese is not considered to be the most important language for trade. There are a number of reasons for this. Firstly, many Portuguese and Spanish understand each other without needing to speak each other's language. Secondly, since Portugal is a well established market, it is possibly seen as less important to concentrate efforts there, as it is for example, with Britain or Germany, where languages cause more problems. The predominance of English is not only apparent as the languages of the UK and USA, but there is also strong evidence of English as the lingua franca of trade with Germany, Denmark, the Netherlands and Norway. Furthermore, for those companies exporting to Japan or South East Asia, for example, business dealings are almost invariably conducted in English.

Other significant variables

There is evidence that language usage is associated with companies of a particular size (in terms of employees and turnover) and share of exports.

Figure 5: Language use by size of company

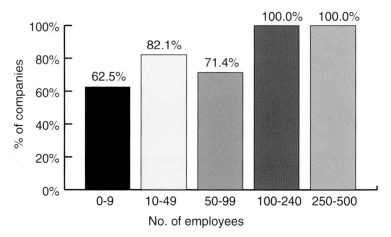

For example, all companies with over 100 employees indicated that they used language skills in the workplace, whereas those with fewer than 100 employees did not (Fig. 5). The larger the company, the more likely it is to have staff able to use languages, as well as the market need to do so.

Figure 6: Language use by turnover

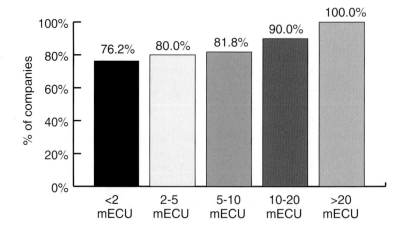

As in the *FLAIR* report, there is also evidence of a correlation between turnover and language use. As companies increase turnover, their use of languages is likely to grow: 100% of companies with a turnover of 20 m ECU or more will use languages, which falls to 76% where turnover is less than 2 m ECU – (Fig. 6).

Figure 7: Language use by % exports

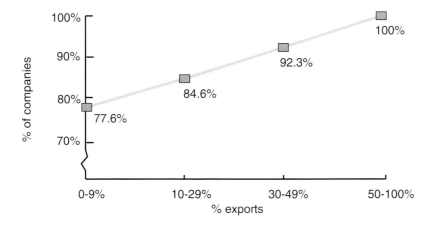

Predictably, there is a direct relationship between volume of exports as a percentage of output and use of languages (Fig. 7) which reaffirms the findings in *FLAIR* (1993). There is also a strong correlation between sector and use of languages. For example, in the Hotel and Catering Industry, 93% of respondents confirmed that languages were used and in the Engineering and Metal Manufacturing Industry a total of 90% of the companies answering the question said that they used languages. The Food, Drink and Tobacco industry only came up with a total of 67%, which is surprising since it is a major exporter. However, language use here was lower than in the less traditional Mineral Extraction and Chemicals industry, which had a total of 91% confirming that foreign languages were used. The Textile industry also recorded 90% usage rate.

Which language skills do companies use?

Table 1: Language skills used (n=124)

Language	Listening/Speaking	Reading	Writing	Culture
English	70.2%	69.4%	66.1%	24.2%
French	47.6%	48.4%	43.5%	18.5%
German	15.3%	13.7%	12.1%	3.2%
Italian	11.3%	11.3%	7.3%	4.0%
Portuguese	10.5%	11.3%	6.5%	5.6%

Listening to, and speaking, in English is significantly ahead of all other languages (70.2%), but only fractionally higher than *reading* in English. *Writing* closely follows this but, surprisingly, *culture* is only mentioned by fewer than 1 in 4 companies. By comparison, French skills are used by a third fewer companies (47.6%) than English, but *reading* French and knowledge of French *culture* are proportionally more widely needed, suggesting greater use of written French for communication and, perhaps, greater awareness of French cultural barriers. Also French business contacts tend to have spoken Spanish. Although Portugal is the major export market for many companies surveyed, language use is surprisingly small: the language does not seem to pose any particular barrier, nor is the need great to speak the language.

When companies were asked to identify significant usage, English and French are much closer together underlining the frequency of cross-border contact between France and Spain.

Table 2: Significant Usage of Skills (n=124)

Language	Listening/Speaking	Reading	Writing	Culture
English	15.3%	15.3%	12.1%	2.4%
French	12.1%	8.9%	9.7%	1.6%
German	4.0%	3.2%	4.0%	0.8%
Italian	3.2%	2.4%	2.4%	0.8%

Correspondence, using the telephone, meetings, negotiations and *travelling abroad* are the most frequently cited functions or situations where a foreign language is most likely to be used (Fig. 8). Individual languages follow the same pattern. For example, the use of English in the office for speaking on the telephone and handling correspondence attracts a high proportion of the overall percentage, 19% and 20% respectively, along with travel (15%), negotiating (12%) and meetings (15%). In the case of Fashion S.A. speaking French over the phone with French agents led to the development of a very prosperous relationship and invaluable market feedback (see panel):

CASE STUDY: FASHION S.A., Salamanca

Fashion SA manufactures women's clothing such as overcoats, shoes and jackets. The company uses a high proportion of fabrics and clothing materials, such as cashmere and angora, pure wool, as well as wool mixes. When the company made the decision to export to Europe they had to decide which countries to target as the most accessible for export; France was selected.

Language activity
Since there was no-one with sufficient mastery of French it was decided to use local French representatives who would make the initial contact with the customer. This could only be a temporary arrangement and it became very clear that language skills were needed. Some company staff already had some background in a language, so private lessons were organised

for the 2 or 3 who would be needed to keep in contact with the representatives. The second step was to hire people with skills in the foreign languages. This was needed (i) to maintain the contact with France; and (ii) to prepare company for future export markets.

Solving the language barrier

In the past, customers did not contact the company directly because they knew there was nobody who could understand them. When they realised - following the new strategy - there were people who understood French, they began to call directly. French sales representatives started to develop a relationship with Fashion S A and realised that it was much easier to communicate by telephone than it would have been by fax. This new relationship was a distinct advantage for both the customer and the local representatives. For example, there was one customer in Paris who used to speak a little Spanish; when he realised that there was someone who could speak French, he started calling quite frequently, especially for clarification. He rang to discuss colour, style and design. As a result, he became a friend, rather than just a business contact, and this relationship has served as a model for all potential customers.

One striking discovery is the small percentage given to *socialising* across all languages. One reason for this is the perception, in Spain, that social interaction is not strictly seen as a means of doing business, and, thus, the need to speak a foreign language is seen as less important in this situation.

Figure 8: Situations when languages are used

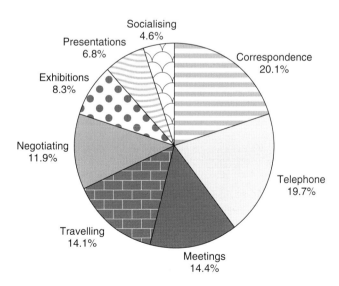

(as % of total occurences)

Language and cultural barriers

Which companies face language barriers?

Figure 9: Languages causing barriers

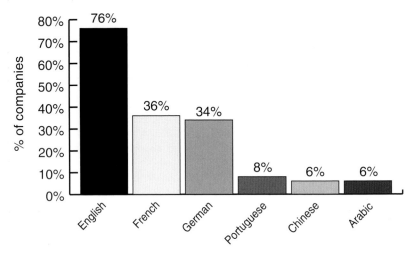

(n=50) (as % of companies with language barriers)

In total, 40% of the sample had experienced language barriers. The language causing the most difficulty is English (76%) (Fig. 9), followed by French with a much lower figure of 36%, and then German with a total of 34%. The group of lesser used languages such as Portuguese (8%), Chinese (6%), Italian (4%) and Japanese and Russian (4% each) are noticeably lower. The findings reaffirm a pattern of need which is not directly related to export destinations since Portugal does not feature prominently.

Is sector significant in companies facing barriers?

In Table 3 the subset of companies facing barriers belong to a specific pattern of sectors: 'other' manufacturing industry (67%), textiles (50%), food drink and tobacco (43%), distribution, hotel and catering (43%), and Engineering and Metal Manufacture (16%). Notably, manufacturing and textiles seem the hardest hit since 50%, or more, positive respondents declared they faced a barrier.

Table 3: Language barriers by sector

Sector	%
Other manufacturing industries	66.7%
Textile industry	50.0%
Food, drink and tobacco industry	43.3%
Distribution, hotel and catering	42.9%
Building and civil engineering	33.3%
Other services	33.3%
Paper and paper products	33.3%
Mineral extraction and chemicals	27.3%
Engineering and metal manufacture	15.8%
Sector summary	
Service	36.4%
Manufacturing/Industry	41.2%

The textile industry, for example, has been under threat from increasing numbers of third world exporters with lower labour costs. It has had to diversify product and market outlets and incorporate new design and production techniques with new materials in order to survive. The squeeze of its traditional markets has obviously left it seeking new overseas markets for which it lacks the necessary skills and knowledge.

Language barriers by size of company

Figure 10: Language barriers by size of company

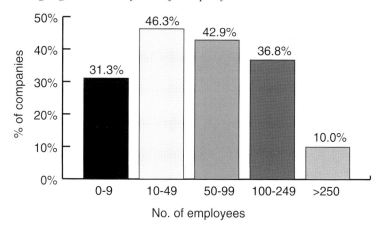

   The general principle holds true that the larger the company, the less the likelihood of hitting a language barrier (Fig. 10). The companies which are most likely to encounter barriers fall into the 10-99 employee category, after which point the trend starts to decline. This can be attributed to two particular factors: size and experience of exporting. For example, larger companies have access to greater numbers of experienced and skilled staff. The larger companies also invest heavily in training: 68% of companies with 100-250 employees and 90% with over 250 employees invest in language training. The same hypothesis is equally evident for size by turnover. The larger the turnover, the less likelihood there is of encountering language barriers. A greater percentage of companies with 10-29% of their output devoted to exports face barriers. This confirms a similar trend in other samples; namely, companies seem to face a higher risk of language barriers when exporting only up to 30% of output (Fig. 11).

Figure 11: Language barriers by % exports

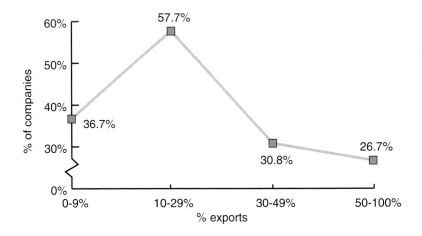

Cultural barriers

Of the 124 companies surveyed, 19% have encountered cultural barriers. The greatest cultural difficulties were with France (29% of those experiencing barriers), Germany (17%) and the UK (8%). Predictably, countries like Hong Kong and Japan, with which Spanish companies have fewer contracts, had a lower rate of cultural barriers (4% each). Cultural differences between Japan and Spain are obviously greater than between France and Spain, but the higher incidence of cultural barriers is accounted for by the increased range and volume of contact. Nonetheless, contact with French culture appears proportionally more problematic than with other nationalities.

Table 4.: Causes of cultural barriers

Culture name	%
Business etiquette	42%
Time and space	42%
Meetings	13%
Business/management style	8%
Social behaviour	4%
Holidays/religion	4%

(n=24) (as % of companies experiencing barriers)

Business etiquette and *time differences* are recognised as the chief causes of cultural barriers, each with 42%. An example of *business etiquette* is entertaining clients and making social conversation. A Spanish company doing business with Germans may find their work ethic more rigid than their own; for instance, Spanish behaviour would be more relaxed over the timing and duration of lunch and dinner compared with the Germans. Differing senses of humour have been cited as causing clashes in Germany, France and Britain. The other major cultural barrier which was acknowledged is perception and *management of time*. For example, a typical Spanish working day starts at around 9.00 a.m. and finishes at approximately 2.00 p.m. and then the afternoon 'shift' would start at 4.00 p.m. and lasts until 8.00 or 9.00 p.m. The British working day is different; lunch is normally one hour instead of 2 or 3, and business people visiting Spanish companies often have difficulty adjusting to the 'late-finish, early-start' syndrome.

Quintin Sanchez S.A. is a good example of a company experiencing difficulties in the Japanese market in selling their meat products. Moreover, they assumed that English was widely spoken and found it did not help in Japan (see panel):

CASE STUDY: QUINTIN SANCHEZ SA, Salamanca

Quintin Sanchez SA is a family company founded some 50 years ago and primarily involved in making hams and sausages in the traditional Iberian style. The raw material is pork meat from Extremadura and Andalucia. The sausages are processed using the highest quality material, which is the lean part of the pork meat from the Bellote, which gives the famous salchichiones and the spicy chorizos sauce.

As soon as African pig disease disappeared in 1990/1 export opportunities opened up for Quintin Sanchez - primarily with countries like France and the UK, since French was easier to acquire and English more widely known. Italy was also accessible, since they already knew the type of product and Italian was similar to Spanish. Major barriers existed in Japan where the main difficulty was the time taken travelling there, then knowing enough culture and language to make it possible to introduce the products into people's homes. Elsewhere in Europe the main difficulties encountered did not arise on a country level, but on a regional level for example, in the Flemish speaking areas of Belgium.

The suitability of the product was not the issue but the fact that most people did not understand any language, other than Flemish. This was also true in ports of Spain, in Catalonia and the Basque country, where the company had to bring out catalogues in the local languages. Once the material was translated the company found it much easier to sell. Currently, the company operates in three languages: English, French and Spanish.

Future strategy

Quinton Sanchez SA is currently looking for language solutions that would make it possible to communicate in all countries. The first stage has been to appoint people who are willing to work abroad for the company, either as translators or as commercial agents, who understand that there is now only one large unique global market. Their greatest surprise, however, was to discover how few people spoke English in Japan and they found themselves having to rely on pocket machine translators as the only means of communication, which was obviously not ideal but better than nothing.

Other significant factors

The major difference between the types of company facing language and cultural barriers is that more companies from the service sector encounter cultural barriers (23%). This could be due to the fact that there is a greater need to understand clients' personal preferences in the service sector. For example, selling car hire, or financial services, requires far greater understanding of the local culture since both have to be tailored to individual need and local buying patterns.

Size of company continues to be a factor: again, companies with 50-99 employees are likely to face the greatest prospect of meeting cultural barriers.

Lost business

Of the 124 companies that answered this section of the questionnaire, 19% confirmed that they had experienced a loss of business due to the lack of language or cultural knowledge.

Table 5: Reasons for lost business

Reason for losing business	%
Inability to communicate (effectively)	26%
Exhibitions and trade fairs	13%
Misunderstandings	9%
Errors in translations/interpreting	9%
Can't capitalise on opportunities	9%
Phone and switchboard	4%
Enquiries not followed-up	4%
Problems with agents and distributors	4%

(n=23) (as % of companies that lost business)

As indicated in Table 5, 26% of the companies confirmed that they believed that their loss of business was due to the inability to *'communicate effectively'*, followed by *'exhibitions'* and *'trade fairs'*, *'misunderstandings'*, *'errors in translations/ interpreting'* and not being able to *'capitalise on opportunities'*. Some of the explanations for this loss of business are that, in the case of *misunderstandings*, companies said that there had been mistakes in understanding leading to wrong actions or misplaced emphasis, or ambiguity in agreements. In the case of companies *failing to capitalise on opportunities*, the reasons given were that it was not always possible to speak directly to the right person and so take advantage of the opportunity without knowledge of the local language and culture[2].

When the companies were followed-up, many responded about potential loss of business, rather than actual. Therefore, in many cases the loss they were describing was perceived and not quantifiable. In the same survey in France and Germany, companies were able to quantify the actual loss of business, which was directly related to the lack of linguistic or cultural knowledge. Some companies appear more vulnerable than others. For example, the sectors where most potential business is lost are: *distribution; hotel and catering; food, drink and tobacco; engineering and metal manufacture*. Smaller companies are most likely to lose business; especially those with a turnover of less than 10m ECU p.a..

Translation problems are illustrated by the case of Construcciones Electricas Olmedo S.A., an electrical equipment manufacturer in Salamanca. Their contract translators could not cope with the text for transformer operation plates and they were forced to fall back on their own specialist knowledge (see panel):

CASE STUDY: CONSTRUCCIONES ELECTRICAS OLMEDO S.A., Electrical Equipment Construction, Salamanca

Construcciones Electricas Olmedo S.A. is a family company founded in the late 50's. Originally, it was basically a repair shop which, as the years went by, transformed into a manufacturing unit producing transformers for distribution and power. It now employs 34 people and exports to France, Germany and Latin America. Its products are used for the transformation and transport of energy generated by power-stations directly to users by high tension power lines.

Export plans

The company is currently expanding in Europe. At this early stage, contact with these countries is carried out through specialised intermediaries, such as translation companies. It has recognised that this is no longer wholly appropriate and it has been decided that part of the staff, namely the technical and commercial staff, should be trained in foreign languages, starting with English (but later French and German). The company has taken the view that the next generation of people joining the company will have not only have to be able to express themselves in English, but also in other languages, to ensure more effective commercial communication.

Evidence of language barriers: translation problems

The company has realised the shortcomings of just using translation companies as the principal intermediaries with clients. The company has taken the view that it is losing business opportunities since open communication is not being established with the potential customers about the products. Most of the time, what translation companies do is transfer a text from Spanish into the other language without transferring the spirit, or real sense, of what the producer wishes to see transmitted. For instance, when they export transformers they have to become familiar with the required documentation in order to respond to the specific needs of the customer. This was the case when they exported transformers to the French market and had to produce all the documentation in French, as stated in the customer's specification. In this case, the company found itself having to carry out the translation of the technical description on the transformer operation plate since the translation company had no knowledge of the technical terms used for transformers.

Evidence of lost business

Not having staff qualified in English and French has made the company less competitive and prevented it from expanding the volume of exports to those markets. Currently, the percentage of exports in the company is very low and, if after years of experience it has recognised it is essential to speak the customer's language. It has not been possible to give a presentation in their own language, Spanish, since foreign customers always prefer to hear their own language, and not the language of the supplier or the manufacturer.

Future options

The managing director believes that the only real long term solution lies with education. Language barriers are partly a generation issue since, for instance, many young people have either visited or even lived in foreign countries and do not accept the inevitability of non-communication, but instead recognise the importance of personal communication as a result of the contact they have already experienced. He recognises that the current generation of Spanish managers generally know only Spanish and little else, which has become a major commercial drawback.

Language training

In total, 36% of the companies surveyed indicated that they had undertaken language training and 78% of these said it had improved their performance. English is clearly seen as the most important target for training followed by French, German and Portuguese. Only a small percentage of the total sample (5%) indicated having used new methodology in their training, such as CD-ROM or other computer-based training (CBT). Most of the companies using the new methodology also confirmed it was effective. Moreover, 82% of the companies that had undertaken language training in the last three years agreed they needed training in the future; 62% stated that they did not experience language barriers; and only 38% stated that they did. This suggests that companies perceive language training in a commercial context to be more effective than not as a means of reducing barriers.

Figure 12: Past training by language

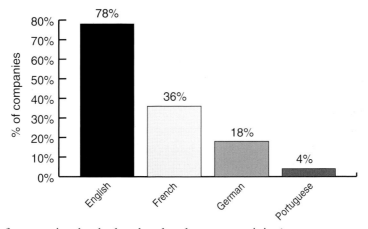

(as % of companies that had undertaken language training)

Figure 13: Past training by size of company

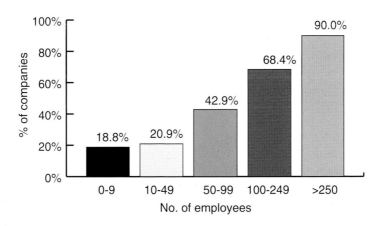

The larger the company, the more training is likely to be undertaken; while 21% of companies with 0-49 employees had undertaken training in the past, 43% of companies with between 50-99 employees acknowledged they had trained staff. But the largest companies, those with over 250 employees, had a 90% training rate. Larger companies not only have the resources but are also willing to invest in language training. There is clearly a link between recognition of the value of language training and avoidance of language barriers. For example, two thirds of companies exporting between 30-49% of output have undertaken language training. It is below this threshold that difficulties seem to arise.

It appears that companies in certain sectors are more aware of communication barriers due to the nature of their trade. Companies in distribution, hotel and catering, and food, drink and tobacco have invested more heavily in language training. Many companies do, however, acknowledge that the training may have been misplaced within the organisation. Respondents indicated that they did not receive regular training and that training was offered only when a specific problem arose. A number of companies in the survey agreed there was a need to incorporate training strategies into their export plans but they were not clear on how to go about it.

Future demand for language skills

A majority of companies (60%) confirmed they did intend to start trading with foreign countries in the future. The countries that the Spanish companies planned to trade with were principally in Europe; in particular, France and Portugal, but also the USA, Canada and the Far East.

Two thirds of the companies confirmed that they would need language training in the next three years: 59% of the sample stated that English was the language in which future training would be needed, followed by French and German with 32% and 18%, respectively. Of the companies that needed training, 84% had employees with language skills, 47% had experienced language barriers and 45% had undertaken training in the past.

Analysis of future language requirements

Companies that had undertaken language training and/or recognised the need for language training in the future, did not experience as many problems with language barriers: this confirms the existence of 'language-aware' companies which take action, often when they reach a certain size, or attain a particular export profile. Smaller companies are most at risk, especially those with fewer than 100 employees and exporting less than 30% of output.

However, knowledge of foreign languages in the world of international commerce today is no longer a question of choice, it has become a necessity if the company is to grow and succeed. Successful exporting companies can no longer afford to ignore the link between language expertise and export growth.

Notes

1. see Methodology chapter

2. Quotations on Lost Business

- At several sales because they sent an English catalogue
- We do not take part/attend international Trade Fairs due to lack of language skills therefore we do not do all the selling
- Due to lack of languages we cannot successfully close commercial deals
- In business with Middle Eastern countries where they prefer to use their own language
- It is possible. At trade fairs and exhibitions it is not the same for a translator to express the qualities of a product as for company
- We have lost more than one business opportunity due to the lack of language skills so it is very important
- Difficulty in responding correctly and with ease to questions from the clients - especially when the client faces
- Because we cannot explain our production technique and the artistic objective of our work
- In Germany, GM, VW and Ford require someone who is fluent in German
- It is impossible to negotiate with companies due to the lack of knowledge of English
- It is difficult to calculate if we have suffered an operational loss due to the lack of language skills but I suppose so
- Due to misunderstandings brought on by a lack of language skills
- Thai people visited the wine merchant and they did not like to have a translator because they spoke English
- Possible lost contacts at Trade Fairs

6 The Language and Communication Needs of French Export Companies in the Poitou-Charentes Region

Francois Marchessou, Isabelle Guérineau & Stephen Hagen

Background

The *Elucidate* study of French companies gives important insights into how languages are used in a sample of 245 international SMEs (with fewer than 500 employees) based in and around Poitou-Charentes (see Chapter 2). Though the sample is limited to this region, the study adds greatly to our existing knowledge of findings from other French surveys and, more importantly, measures the growing impact of internationalisation on cross-border communication demands in a sample of French SMEs in the mid-to late 90s.

Earlier French studies

The 90s have seen very few large-scale empirical studies of foreign language use in French companies. The most relevant, *'Les Besoins en Langues Etrangères' (Cariou, B. & Le Gall, F., 1993)*, surveyed a similar number of companies (251) with a similar profile to *Elucidate*, but in the Brittany area. The latter, *FLAIR-France*, led by Stephen Hagen, was carried out by the Institut Universitaire de Technologie in Brest in association with the *Centre International d'Etudes des Langues* as part of the LINGUA Programme's *Foreign Language Analysis in Regions of Europe* Project 1993 (for details see Appendix 1 of the *FLAIR* report in Hagen (ed.) 1993: 103-107). Both *FLAIR* and *Elucidate* have produced comparable sets of data on language usage, language and cultural barriers, as well as training and translation needs. This can also be set in the broader context of language skills in the French population at large, reported in Expolangues-Ipsos Europe (Dec. 1996).

Major comparisons with FLAIR

Comparing the key findings of *FLAIR* and *Elucidate*, the number of companies identifying barriers appears to have risen from 1 in 5 in 1993 (*FLAIR*, 1993: 17) to over 1 in 3 in 1996, though the actual number of businesses which have lost known business opportunities as a direct result of a language/cultural barrier is closer to 1 in 8. This apparent growth is probably due to the greater internationalisation of French companies. Other relevant differences include:

- a rise in the importance of German (followed by Spanish) as the second language most widely used after English (reflecting the predominant position of Germany as the leading export market);

- little change in the level of implementation of language strategies; an almost identical proportion of companies in both studies (ca. 25%) indicate they have a language strategy (but 75% do not);

However, growth in advertising without evidence of an increase in language strategies suggests a short-term response rather than long-term planning. This is borne out in *'Entreprises et Carrières'* (Le Nagaro, G. (1997)): *'there is no strong set of doctrines regarding foreign languages within SMEs and languages are not at the forefront of their preoccupations'*. Certainly, management and marketing skills still seem to be divorced from language competence in the minds of executives. This lack of recognition is also apparent from data on language training: only 11% of companies in the above survey with an existing language training programme intended to invest in further training within the following 12 months, whereas 38% wished to make their staff more computer-literate and 35% wanted to develop greater awareness of quality. Training is not therefore seen as a company's primary route to achieving linguistic competence. Further evidence confirms that many companies look instead to hiring native speakers, particularly in the case of German, as a primary tactic to address language problems.

One example of this is the paradox alluded to in an article published in *Moniteur du Commerce International* ('MOCI') (Deysine, A.(1997)). While lip-service is still paid to language training as the obvious means of overcoming language problems in company philosophy, hiring native speakers appears to be the actual means of doing so. Most companies in the study look to education for the improvement in the language skills of young people as the means of addressing their own needs in the longer term.

Some justification for this apparent confidence in the educational system is borne out in the *Expolangues-Ipsos* Europe study, where the French are doing comparatively well at language learning. For example, they have the highest proportion of young people (15-34 yrs) who claim to speak at least one other language: 79% compared with 74% for Italy and 72% for Germany. They also have the highest proportion across all ages, 61%, compared with 49% in Germany and 44% in Britain (E-I, p10).

Which languages do companies use?

General overview

Twice as many companies use English as German or Spanish, confirming its dominant position (see Fig. 1). When companies are asked to indicate which language is the most important to their business (Fig. 2), English rises even more significantly in importance. Nine times as many companies rank English as most important, compared with German, which, in turn, is considered most important by twice as many companies as Spanish.

Table 1: Languages used*		Table 2: Importance of each		Table 3: No. of languages used	
English	83%	English	73%	At least 1	87%
German	44%	German	8%	2	63%
Spanish	42%	Spanish	4%	3	33%
Italian	17%	Italian	1%	4	11%
Chinese	2%	Dutch	<1%	5	2%
Portuguese	2%	Portuguese	<1%		
Dutch	2%			*(n=245)*	
Russian	2%				
Japanese	<1%	*survey figures*			
Arabic	<1%	*updated late 1997*			
Czech	<1%				

The predominance of English (Table 1) cannot be explained simply by the volume of trade with English-speaking countries. For example, the principal export destinations of the region are: Germany (31%), Spain, Italy, Belgium, the UK (all in the range of 10%-20%), the USA (8%), Africa (7%) and Japan (5.3%). The concept of a one-to-one relationship between use of a particular language and the local language of trading destinations is not substantiated. Moreover, there has been growth, for example, in the proportion of companies using several languages rather than one (see Table 3) which tends to support the view that trade increasingly requires multilingual capability. In Table 3 a significant proportion of companies (nearly 2 out of 3) use two languages, a third use three and about 1 in 10 use at least four. English may be the *lingua prima* of world trade, but it is, by itself, no longer adequate for global trading.

Interestingly, only 76% of export companies claimed to use one language in *FLAIR*, compared with 87% in *Elucidate*. *Elucidate* also shows a greater diversity of languages in use than *FLAIR* with the notable addition of Chinese, Japanese and Czech.

How representative is this sample?

The above findings partly reflect the *Expolangues-Ipsos* poll results which show that English is predominant (47% of French people claim some knowledge). However, Spanish is second (26%) and German (16%) third. With regard to 'fluency' (or full competency) twice as many speak English (23%) compared with Spanish (11%), which is approximately double that of German (6%). *Elucidate* confirms the far greater significance of German for business people.

Which language skills are widely used in trade?

The skills that seem to be the most important are *speaking/listening* and reading as far as English and Spanish are concerned, while *reading* is slightly higher than *speaking/ listening* for German (Table 4). The higher rate noted for Spanish *listening/speaking* compared with German is largely due to the greater availability of Spanish speakers in French management. More than twice as many managers speak Spanish well, compared with German.

Table 4: Language skills used

(n=245)

Language	Listening/Speaking	Reading	Writing	Cullture
English	77.6%	72.7%	69.0%	20.0%
Spanish	36.3%	32.7%	28.2%	7.8%
German	35.1%	35.9%	32.7%	9.4%
Italian	14.3%	11.8%	9.8%	2.0%
Portuguese	2.4%	1.6%	1.6%	0.8%
Dutch	2.0%	2.0%	2.0%	0.4%
Russian	1.6%	0.8%	0.8%	0.8%
Chinese	1.6%	0.4%	0.4%	2.0%
Czech	0.4%	0.4%	0.4%	0.4%
Arabic	0.4%	0.4%	0.4%	
Japanese				0.8%

Perception of the importance of culture as a separate 'skill', or competence, is present for most languages. Though less significant than might be expected, it still applies to 1 in 5 companies using English, 1 in 10 for German and approximately 1 in 12 for Spanish. Not unexpectedly, recognition of the importance of understanding culture is proportionally greater for Chinese. The relatively lower value may, however, signify lower awareness rather than the absence of a problem.

Figure 4 shows that languages are predominantly used by secretarial and administrative staff, rather than by management. This is true for all languages with the exception of Spanish (Table 5), largely thanks to its dominance in the school system. In the sub-set of companies using Spanish, for example, there is a higher percentage of 'school educated' Spanish-speaking staff than staff trained through regular classes. At face value there would appear to be a mismatch between school provision and business need.

Figure 4: Employees with language skills by position

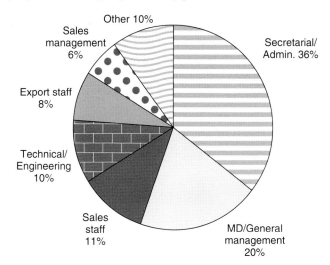

(as % of employees with language skills)

Table 5: Language skills by function and language

Function	German (n=69)*	Spanish (n=68)	Italian (n=20)	English (n=276)
Secretarial/Admin.	42%	25%	45%	37%
MD/General management	13%	28%	15%	20%
Technical/Engineering	6%	10%		11%
Sales staff	13%	15%	15%	9%
Sales management	7%	4%	10%	6%
Export staff	12%	12%	10%	6%
Finance/Accounts		6%		5%
Export management	3%		5%	4%
Marketing/PR	1%			1%
Purchasing staff	3%			1%

(as % of employees with German language skills)

Twice as many French managers speak Spanish than speak German, which reflects the national picture (*Expolangues-Ipsos*, p.13). On the other hand, a greater proportion of secretaries/administrators than managers have German skills, which was also the case in *FLAIR* (Hagen, 1993: 105). It seems that, (thanks to the place of Spanish in the curriculum), many more managers can lift the phone and chat in Spanish, but are obliged to give their secretaries the task of sending a fax to Germany.

Available language skills - profile of employees

Approximately half the employees with language skills are either at basic (34%) or *intermediate* levels (15%) (Fig.5). Language skills are most commonly found amongst secretarial and administrative staff, however 44% of these have only a basic knowledge. By contrast, all export managers have advanced or fluent knowledge, which is accounted for partly by the presence of native speakers reflecting the growing evidence of an international workforce.

Figure 5: Employees with language skills by level of competence

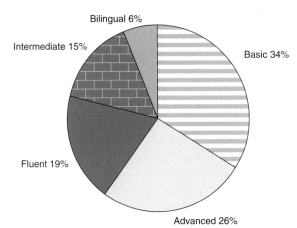

(as % of employees with language skills)

This is particularly true for German; for example, over 1 in 5 employees with German skills are native speakers (Table 6). Otherwise, the preferred method of developing language skills in the workforce tends to be part-time regular classes for German (43%), English (38%) and Spanish training (24%). Surprisingly few employees (22%) acquired their knowledge of English from school.

Table 6: Language skills by education

Language	German* (n=28)	Spanish (n=25)	English (n=114)
Part-time regular	43%	24%	38%
School educated	7%	28%	22%
Intensive	4%	16%	15%
University educated	25%	16%	14%
Lived abroad	–	4%	6%
Native speaker	21%	8%	4%
Self-tuition	–	4%	2%

(as % of employees with German language skills)

Which situations require language use?

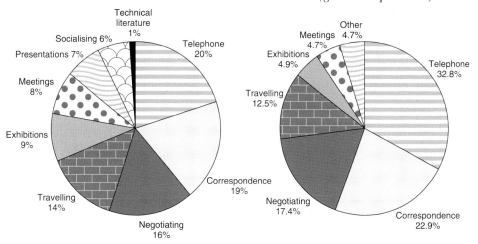

Figure 6: Situations when languages used

Figure 7: Situations ranked 1 (greater importance)

(as % of total occurrences)

The telephone is by far the most important medium for cross-border communication (Fig. 6). *Telephoning, correspondence and negotiating* all predominate (Fig. 7), denoting their relatively more important function in international business.

New technology – in the form of ICT – is also starting to make an impact. In the case of Alliance Pastorale, a partnership of stock breeders in Montmorillon, the economic as well as advertising, value of the company's new website has been significantly enhanced leading to a significant increase in sales leads (see panel):

CASE STUDY: ALLIANCE PASTORALE, Montmorillon

Alliance Pastorale has been in existence for 60 years and employs 70 people. It comprises a professional body of stock breeders and is situated in Montmorillon (8000 inhabitants) 350 km south-west of Paris and 50 km from Poitiers.

The company sells breeding and husbandry equipment (fencing materials, specialised vehicles, animal feeding materials) to breeders and also carries out biological laboratory analyses to identify disease. They respond to telephone queries from livestock breeders all over the world concerning a range of activity from high-tech artificial insemination to halal slaughtering techniques. For some time now the Manager who has had a medium level command in English, has called upon interpreters when needed. This solution, however, was not particularly suitable, as he believed it to be increasingly vital to create the proper "business atmosphere" through direct communication.

Their own on-site "International" service within the company was created in 1996 after a trilingual (English, Arabic, French) engineer was recruited. When it was realised there was an important lack of sheep in Muslim areas, the company decided to target Muslim countries. The creation of an English website was the first action taken, which immediately opened up relations with other new countries. The site receives an average of 300 visits a month.

Analysis of language strategy

The Managing Director believes that, for a small investment, the website site produces an enormous increase in the number of contacts with foreign countries. The website has lead the company to:

- recruit a Website manager able to combine fluent spoken and written English with a good knowledge of the company's area of activity.

- develop the use of English as a company language, especially for telephone communication.

Conclusion

For the Managing Director, use of the Internet, and a website, and the ability to communicate in English are the two corner-stones of an export strategy for a rural company. A formula which would allow employees to attend training courses still needs to be found, since many workers are freelance and do not have any free time for this. They would also be unable to travel to lessons offered 50 km away.

Is trade being lost for lack of language or cultural competence?

Language barriers

Over a third of companies in the *Elucidate* sample (35%) claim to have encountered linguistic barriers. The languages causing barriers are dominated by the main European languages, as expected, however, Far Eastern languages such as Chinese (7%) and Japanese (5%) also create problems (Fig. 8).

Figure 8: Languages causing barriers

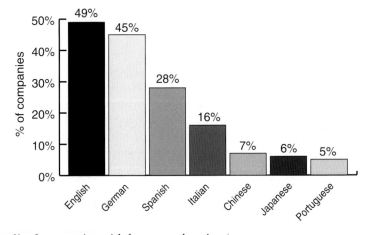

(n=86) (as % of companies with language barriers)

Figure 9: Situations causing barriers

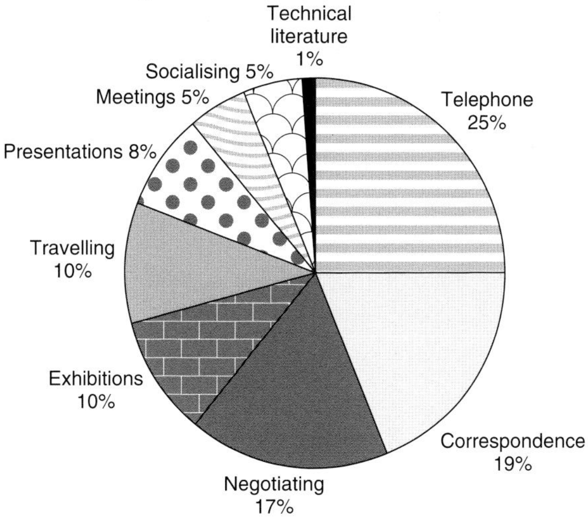

(as % of total occurrences)

In Fig. 9 the highest number of linguistic problems arise from use of the *telephone* (25%), *correspondence* (19 %) or *negotiations* (17 %). As one might expect, problems arise in the main areas of usage. However, *negotiating* is a relatively greater source of barriers since the opportunity for misunderstanding is more significant.

This is particularly true in the context of cultural misunderstanding: 8% of companies encountered cultural obstacles, with 40% of these quoting *negotiating* as the main reason.

Cultural barriers

Japan, followed by Germany, appears to pose the greatest cultural barriers with the UK much lower down the list (see Figs 10 & 11 below). The kind of issues faced are borne out by SNC Charpentron et Cie, a manufacturer and distributor of cognac. Only when they took advice from a Japanese native speaker did they achieve the lasting success they expected (see panel):

CASE STUDY: SNC CHARPENTRON et Cie, 16200 Gondeville

The company is a family-run business, situated 15 km from Cognac, and carries out two lines of business activity:

- the manufacturing of spirits (cognac, pineau);
- the distribution, both of their own products and those of other companies.

Exports used to be confined to Belgium, but since 1979 they export to 12 countries.

The language strategy

When the company started exporting further afield, it did not have the resources to recruit additional staff merely for linguistic reasons.

Instead, the company hired translators through the Chamber of Commerce. A freelance was found who was able to carry out translations in English, German and Spanish which were then checked for quality control by a professional translation office, which also processes the more complex enquiries. However, the company's language strategy has progressed more from the foreign contacts that it has made and their advice and recommendations than through translators.

Success in Japan

At a trade fair, Charpentron met a Japanese woman who, by chance, was working on the export of Limoges porcelain products. Her advice on the translation of documents destined for Japan proved essential.

As a result of the advice on the cultural and linguistic adaptation:

- Product names and document content were changed for the Japanese market.

- Product brochures and leaflets were changed and re-edited into four languages: French, German, English and Japanese.

- The company put into place a network of local commercial agents in each country who were contracted to contact all customers two to three times a year.

- Financial and language resources are pooled at foreign exhibitions.

- The recruitment of the agents took place through personal recommendation. The company now works in collaboration with a champagne merchant and one for Bordeaux wine, which allows each of the three business partners to increase their direct contact with clients.

- The company has now hired four French-speaking salespeople for the French market.

- Expert information, which is traditionally transferred by fax (in 90% of the cases), will be conveyed by email located on a new company website, which is now a must with Asian markets. The website was prepared in time for "Vinexpo" which took place in Hong Kong, in June 1998. Early indications have shown that this site will offer a gigantic boost to cross-border communication, and that it will become the main medium of communication with customers.

- The availability of this culturally-adapted information brought about a marked increase in the number of customers, within six months from initial release.

Figure 10: Cultural obstacles by country

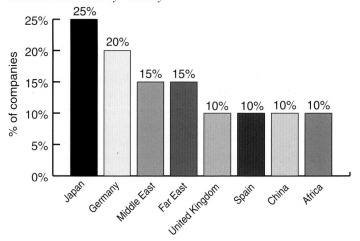

(as % of companies that experienced barriers)

Figure 11: Context for cultural barrier

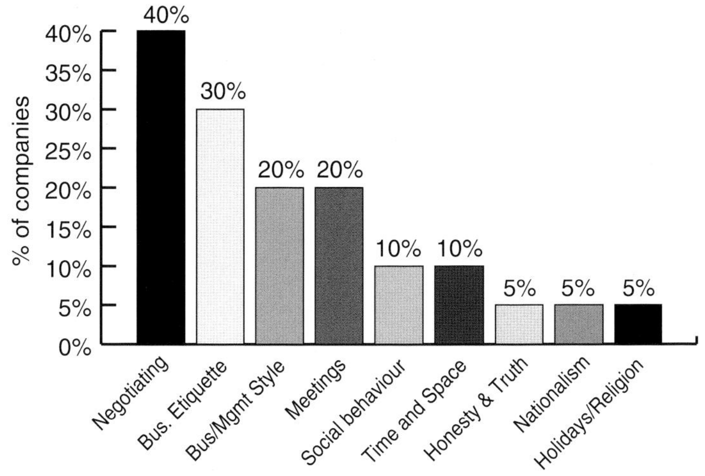

(as % of companies that experienced barriers)

The small number of responses (n=20) do not enable us to draw many significant conclusions. On the other hand, comments by the respondents themselves give a significantly greater insight:

- *Germany:* 'some disagreement on the notion of safety and responsibility; lack of tolerance for conversations on trifling subjects and overblown words and phrases.'

- *Japan/Asia:* 'deeper problems connected to different social codes which have to be known in order to carry out exchanges.'

- *Middle East:* 'religion, timetables, reliability of payments.'

- *Britain, Spain:* 'different approaches to the ways of carrying out negotiations.'

What are the causes of lost business?

Self-evidently, SMEs which are more experienced exporters and already use languages are less likely to encounter difficulty. So, SMEs that have experienced CEOs aged over 40 and with over 250 employees tend not to encounter as many barriers. On the other hand, micro-enterprises with fewer than 10 staff, frequently report difficulty. Volume of exports is also a significant factor. Companies that export between 0% and 29% of output seem to experience the greatest linguistic problems, while companies which export more than 50% face fewest difficulties. This supports the hypothesis of a threshold (Hagen, 1993:94) and also broadly reflects the profile of French SMEs most likely to use languages, namely:

- \> 100 – < 500 employees
- 10 – 20 m ECU turnover
- exporting 10% – 29% of output

In other words, companies exporting under a third of their output are more likely to face a language barrier because they are often entering new, untried territory and tend to be moving into a more proactive exporting mode, away from the low turnover, reactive category.

The 13% of companies with evidence of lost business cited the following reasons:

- problems with the telephone
- lack of confidence expressing oneself in a foreign language
- inability to respond to enquiries or to derive significant benefit from business opportunities
- inability to participate in fairs and exhibitions abroad
- misunderstandings (general)
- faulty translations
- problems with salespeople and representatives
- total inability to communicate
- lack of any cultural "common ground".

When classified in order of importance, 'inability to communicate' and 'lack of follow-up' were critical (see Table 7).

Table 7 : Reasons for lost business

Reason for losing business	%
Inability to communicate (effectively)	27%
Enquiries not followed-up	12%
Can't capitalise on opportunities	12%
Exhibitions and trade fairs	9%
Lack of confidence	6%
Phone and switchboard	3%
Misunderstandings	3%

(n=33)   *(as % of companies that lost business)*

21% of companies with between 250-500 employees recognise they lose trade due to cultural or linguistic causes. This figure can be contrasted with companies of 100-249 employees, where lost trade is only 5.6%. This research also shows that the number of missed business opportunities decreases as export volume increases and also that companies with an annual turnover below 10 m ECU are more likely to face the prospect of loss. The risk is higher for industrial companies, than for services.

It is thus possible to identify the type of company most likely to experience linguistic difficulties and target them for aid; they tend to be companies which are already exporting up to a third of output and are medium-sized (250-500 employees, an MD under 40 and a turnover less than 20 m ECU).

It is unlikely that the level of cultural and linguistic difficulties will diminish since 56% of the companies surveyed are contemplating establishing commercial relations with new non French-speaking countries and over half expect to need language training programmes within 3 years. However, although company managers think it is obviously better to communicate with customers in their own language, the majority do not believe language obstacles will block a strong export drive and are more affected by the global economic outlook, which has been borne out recently by events in SE Asia.

Some smaller companies, like Minet S.A. in Pampoux, have found ways round language barriers by subcontracting their language needs to companies like Fiduciaire de France, and making sure their local agents speak good French (see panel):

CASE STUDY: MINET SA, Pamproux

Based in the countryside, 40 km from Poitiers, this family-run business manufactures bedroom suites. The company has been in existence for 23 years and employs 30 people. 5% of its production is imported to Reunion Island and the Netherlands, and 13% of its annual purchases are imported.

In September 1994, a representative in the Netherlands was recruited through the Chamber of Commerce. As he only spoke Dutch, and those in charge of the company only speak French, there were a lot of communication problems. The agent soon gave up and ceased to represent the company products. However, the company continued to receive his orders in English by fax, which could therefore not be dealt with.

The arrival of the CEO's son into the company, who was assigned responsibility for export activities, made it possible to develop internal relations.

While studying a two year course in Economics and Business Administration, he studied English a few hours per week. Taking into consideration his insufficient level in the language, he attended private classes at the Chamber of Commerce, 40 km from the company. He attended two hours of instruction each week for twenty five weeks. He is currently trying to continue with his training, despite his lack of free time.

A greater commitment to language issues arose when the CEO's son joined the company and started learning English. At the same time, the company established a contract with "Fiduciaire de France", an accountancy firm which provides an export support service for SMEs and specialises in non-French speaking countries.

The staff of the support service comprises four people, (two of whom are quadrilingual) who contact customers directly, organise trade missions to countries which have some potential for the company and train people for export. They are also in charge of the translation of written documents which they subcontract.

They set up projects in Benelux and the Netherlands for Minet S.A. and help in the selection of French speaking staff from among a group of forty eight agents who have applied from different countries to represent the company.

The contract with the export agency has not yet produced any further increase in turnover, but negotiations currently taking place will undoubtedly lead to further business.

What is the likely future pattern of demand for languages?

Over half the companies in the sample indicated they would require language training before the year 2000. The particular languages identified were:

Figure 12: Future training by language   *Figure 13: Past training by language*

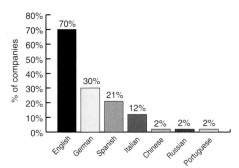

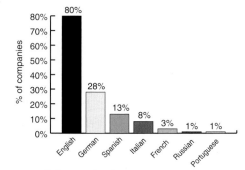

(n=127) (as % of companies requiring training)   *(n=76) (as % of companies with past training)*

Compared with current usage, it is likely that demand for the major European languages will remain in the same proportion as current usage. However, there is evidence of increasing need for the 'marginal' languages such as Chinese and Russian. Yet, training demand will remain significantly higher for English than for other languages, reflecting current levels. (The information in Figures 12 and 13 is expanded in Table 8 overleaf).

Table 8: Language training - past and future demand

	Trained in past		Anticipate future training	
	(n=76)[1]	(n=245)[2]	(n=127)[3]	(n=245)[2]
English	80%	25%	70%	36%
German	28%	9%	30%	16%
Spanish	13%	4%	21%	11%
Italian	8%	2%	12%	6%
Chinese	0	-	2%	1%
Russian	1%	-	2%	1%
Portuguese	1%	-	2%	1%

([1] - as % of companies who have trained in past; [2] - as % of total sample; [3] - as % of companies needing training in future.)

Conclusions

A number of key findings arise from the study:

- key communication interfaces are telephoning and negotiating, which need special emphasis in the preparation of training programmes;

- it is important not to neglect the cultural aspects, since many companies may not be aware of them (those companies with the fewest number of linguistic problems are those which are more aware of cultural obstacles);

- it is important to make companies aware of how much business they would gain from greater linguistic confidence (those companies claiming the most frequent use of languages are also those which recognise they have lost business opportunities through poor command of languages, perhaps due to their greater awareness of the problem).

Bibliography

Brüggemann E. (1995), *Fremdsprachenbedarf der Wirtschaft in der Region Karlsruhe* (Germany: IHK Karlsruhe, 1995).

Cariou, B. & F. Le Gall (1993), *Les Besoins en Langues Etrangères*, IUT Brest in association with Centre International d'Études des Langues (CIEL). Unpublished report, Brest. Summarised in Hagen, S (1993): pp. 103-107.

Castro Calvín, J. (1993), 'Basque Country', Spain. In: Hagen, S. (Ed.), *Languages in European Business : A Regional Survey of Small and Medium-sized companies* (CILT, 1993).

Deysine, A. (1997) 'Maîtriser les langues vivantes: mirage, alibi ou philosophie de vie?', in 'Pour Exporter Mieux, Parlez plus de Langues', *Le Moci* 1270, Jan 30 - Feb 5 1997.

DTI Language Study 1996, unpublished research report prepared for the Department of Trade and Industry by MetraMartech. (DTI JEPD, Kingsgate House, Victoria Street, London).

DTI Language Study 1997 (Unpublished research report prepared for the Department of Trade and Industry by MetraMartech. (DTI JEPD, Kingsgate House, Victoria Street, London).

Expolangues-Ipsos Europe (1996), Principales Conclusions de l'Etude. Ipsos Marketing Systèmes, 99 rue de l'Abbé Groult, 75739 Paris Cedex 15.

FLAIR-EUROPE: A LINGUA Project Report published as Hagen, S. (1993).

Hagen, S. (Ed) (1993) *Languages in European Business: A regional survey of small and medium sized companies.* (CILT, 1993. ISBN 1 874016216).

Hagen, S. (Ed) (1988), *Languages in British Business. An Analysis of Current Needs, Newcastle:* 'Unique' – University of Northumbria Publishers.

Le Nagaro, G. (1997) 'Se Former aux Langues, un Investissement Obligatoire et Rentable', in 'Des besoins exprimés mais rarement satisfaits', *Entreprise et Carrières* No. 372, Jan 28-Feb 3, 1997.

LIBB, Languages in British Business, published as Hagen, S. (Ed), (1988).

Metcalf, H. (1991) *Foreign Language Needs of Business*, Report No. 215, University of Sussex, Institute of Manpower Studies, A project of the Manpower Commentary Programme (Institute of Manpower Studies, 1991).

MetraMartech (see DTI).

National Languages for Export Campaign, A Campaign developed by DTI/JEPD, Department of Trade and Industry, Kingsgate House, 66-74 Victoria Street, London SW1E 6SW, UK. Tel: (UK) 0171 215 4857 Fax: (UK) 0171 215 4856. E-mail: robert.holkham@LOND04.dti.gov.uk

Teleconomy, unpublished research report.

Further Reading

Akoorie, M. and Enderwick, P. (1992), *The International Operations of New Zealand Companies*, Asia Pacific Journal of Management, Vol. 9, pp. 99-117.

Baker, J. (1984), *Foreign Language and Pre-departure Training in US Multinational Firms*, Personnel Administrator, July, pp. 68-72.

Barham, K. (1987), *The Internationalisation of Business and the International Manager*, International Communication Training, July/August, pp. 6-11.

Bjarnarson, A. (1992), 'Export Behaviour of Companies: A Literature Review', Working Paper 92/16, Edinburgh University: Department of Business Studies.

Blackburn, P. (1988), 'Languages in a Multinational Business', in Hagen. S. (Ed), *Languages in British Business: An Analysis of Current Needs.*

Bredin, J. (1990), 'Ciao, Sprechen Sie Francais', *Industry Week*, 16 July, p. 68.

Castro, Alberto de; Gonzalez, Marìa do Pilar; Osório, Antônio (1997), 'Dinâ mica das Qualificaçôes no meio empresarial português (1985-1994)', *Caminhos da Economia Portuguesa in Economia & Prospectiva*, vol. I, n° 1, April/June, Ministério da Economia, pp. 75-88.

Castro Calvín, J. (1992) 'Identification and Analysis of the linguistic foreign language needs of Spanish export businesses' in *Actas I Jornados Internacionales del Inglés Académico*, Techico y Profesional, Universidad de Alcalá de Henares.

Cohen, J. (1990), 'Business Learns to Speak in Tongues', *Management Review*. January, pp. 6-7.

Council of Europe (1996), *Modern Languages: Learning, Teaching, Assessment – A Common European Framework of Reference.* Draft 2 of a Framework proposal. Ref. CC-LANG (95) 5 rev. IV. Strasbourg: Council of Europe.

Cramer, B.A. (1990), 'Developing Competitive Skill. How American Business People Learn Japanese', *Annals, AAPSS,* Vol. 511, September, pp. 85-96.

Dias, José Manuel Graça, (1993) 'Aspectos do Contexto Empresarial Português em Mudança por Efeito da Internacionalização', Vol. V, pp. 1096 in *Encontro de Economistas de LP FEUP,* 5th-8th April 1993.

Dicht, E., Leibold, M., Kolgymayr, G.G., & S. Muller (1990) 'International Orientation as a Precondition for Export Success', *Journal of International Business Studies*, 1st Qtr.

Enderwick, P. and Gray, D. (1993), 'Foreign Languages in International Business: The Case of New Zealand' Journal of Teaching in International Business, Vol. 4 No. 1, pp. 49-68.

Fixman, C.S. (1990), 'The Foreign Language Needs of US-Based Corporations', *Annals, AAPSS*, Vol. 511, September, pp. 25-46.

Gillespie, K. and Folks, W.R. (1985), 'Foreign Language and International Business: The MIBS Program after Ten Years', *Foreign Language Annals*, February, pp. 47-52.

Graham, J. (1988), 'Globally Speaking ...', *Marketing and Media Decisions*, June, p. 160.

Hagen, S. (1998), *Communicating Across Business Cultures: Trade Sectrets of Successful European Companies*. A video training pack development supported by the Leonardo da Vinci programme distributed by InterAct International, (interactinternational@compuserve.com).

Heller, J.E. (1980), 'Criteria for Selecting an International Manager', Personnel, May-June, pp. 47-55.

Hofstede, G. (1980), *Culture's consequences*, London: Sage.

Hofstede, G. (1991), *Cultures and Organisations*, Maidenhead: McGraw Hill.

Holden, N. (1987), 'The Treatment of Language and Linguistic Issues in the Current English-Language International Management Literature', *Multilingua*, Vol. 6 No. 3, pp. 233-46.

Honório, F. (1993) 'A mobilidade geográfica e sócio-profissional induzida pelo sistema de formação profissional', *Estudos de Juventude*, Cadernos do Instituto de Ciências Sociais, Quinta Série, n° 2, 1993.

Inman, M. (1980), 'Foreign Languages and the US Multinational Corporation', The *Modern Language Journal*, Spring, pp. 64-74.

Kapp, S. (1991), 'Selling through a Babel of Tongues', *Business Marketing*, May, pp. 24-6.

Kilpatrick, R. (1984), 'International Business Communication practices', *Journal of Business Communication*, Autumn, pp. 33-45.

Kramer, W. & R. Weiss (1992), 'Fremdsprachen in der Wirtschaft', in *Beitrag zu interkultureller Kompetenz*, Deutscher Instituts-Verlag.

Lambert, R.D. (1990), 'Foreign language Use among International Business Graduates', *Annals, AAPSS*, Vol. 511, September, pp. 47-59.

Lewis, R. (1987), 'Crossing Cultural Boundaries', *Training Officer*, August, pp. 240-2.

Moys, A. (Ed) (1998) *Where are we going with languages?*, London Nuffield Foundation.

Pearson, M. (1989), 'Languages in a Multinational Company', *The Linguist*, Vol. 28 No. 5, pp. 146-7.

President's Commission on Foreign Languages and International Studies (1979), 'Strength through Wisdom: A Critique of US Capability', *Modern Language Journal*, Spring.

Reeves, N.B.R. (1990), 'The Foreign language Needs of UK-based Corporation', *Annals, AAPSS*, Vol. 511, September, pp. 60-73.

Ribeiro, Carlos de Melo, 'Investimento directo estrangeiro e efeitos induzidos em PME' (1997), *Caminhos da Economia Portuguesa in Economia & Prospectiva*, vol. I, n° 3, Oct./Dec., Ministério da Economia, pp. 115–118.

Roxo, Francisco Velez (1991), *Marketing Para que te Quero*, Book and videocassette IAPMEI, Imagem & Comunicâo, October.

Schlegelmilch, B. & A. Ross (1987), 'The Influence of Managerial Characteristics on Different Measures of Export Success', *Journal of Marketing Management*, 3 (2), pp. 145-158.

Schlegelmilch, B. and Crook, J. (1988), 'Firm-level Determinants of Export Intensity', *Managerial and Decision Economics*, Vol. 9, pp. 291-300.

Shipman, A. (1992), 'Talking the Same Languages', *International Management*, June, pp. 69-70.

Singleton-Green, B. (1991), 'Multiple Languages for the Single Market', *Accountancy*, April, p. 29.

Stanley, J. Ingram, D. and Chittick, G. (1989). *The Relationship between International Trade and Linguistic Competence*, Report to the Australian Advisory Council on Languages and Multicultural Education, Australian Government Publishing Service, Canberra.

Stevens, M. (1989), 'Language Exchange', *Marketing (UK)*, 9 November, pp. 53-4.

Swift, J. (1990) 'Marketing Competence and Language Skills: UK Firms in the Spanish Market', *International Business Communications*. Vol. 2 No. 2, pp. 21-6.

Swift, J. (1991), 'Foreign Language Ability and International Marketing', *European Journal of Marketing*, Vol. 25 No. 12, pp. 36-49.

Trompenaars, F. (1993) *Riding the Waves of Culture*, Nicholas Brealey Publishing.

Tung, R. (1990), 'Language Training and Beyond: The Case of Japanese Multinationals', *Annals, AAPSS*, Vol. 511, pp. 97-108.

Turnbull, P. and Cunningham, M. (Eds) (1981), *International Marketing and Purchasing: A Study among Marketing and Purchasing Executives in Five European Countries,* Macmillan, London.

Turnbull, P. and Welham, G. (1985), 'The Characteristics of European Export Marketing Staff', *European Journal of Marketing*, Vol. 19 No. 2, pp. 31-41.

Tyson, S. (1991) 1992: *An Investigation of Strategies for Management Development,* Occasional Paper, SWP 42/91, Human Resources Group, Cranfield School of Management.

Walters, P.G. (1990), 'The Significance of Foreign Language Skills for Initial Entry Positions in International Firms', *Journal of Teaching in International Business*, Vol. 1 No. 3/4, pp. 71-83.

Watts, N. (1986). *Foreign Languages in Exporting*, Department of Modern Languages, Massey University, Palmerston North.

Watts, N. (1992), *The Use of French in Exporting and Tourism*, Department of Modern Languages, Massey University, Palmerston North.

Weilrich, H. and Buhler, D. (1990), 'Training Managers for the Global Market', *Business*, July/September, pp. 40-3.

Weiss, R. (1992) see Kramer, W. & R. Weiss, 1992.

Appendix

Survey of Foreign Language and Cultural Needs of British Businesses

Could you please answer the questions below in relation to your firm's activities. If you are a subsidiary or branch, please give answers relating to your branch. Thank You.

1.0 About Your Firm

In this survey we need to compare firms of different size and activity. The information from this section is for statistical purposes only; **the identity of individual firms will be confidential.**

1.1 Name of Firm:	
1.2 Address:	
	Postcode
1.3 Telephone No.:	**Fax No.:**
1.4 Your Name:	
1.5 Your Function:	

1.6 Is this firm a subsidiary or branch?   YES [ ]   NO [ ]

If YES, would you please indicate where your head office is located:

Town: **Country:**

1.7 Main Product/Service:				
1.8 Approx. Number of years trading:				
1.9 Approx. No. of employees in firm:				
1.10 Approx. Turnover in £'000 (last financial year):				
1.11 Age band of M.D. (✓)	**20s**	**30s**	**40s**	**50s**	**60s**

1.12 Please indicate:

(a) the approximate percentage of your sales abroad (i.e. exports) :   %

(b) your major export markets. Please circle : Fr. Ger. Sp. Jap. USA. Scand. Rus.

others (please add)_____

(c) the approximate percentage of your purchases bought abroad (i.e. imports) :   %

1.13 Does your firm have an in-house language strategy?   YES [ ]   NO [ ]

If YES, give examples:

(e.g. all reports are in English)   _____

_____

2.0   Current Use of Foreign Languages In Your Firm

The purpose of this section is to help schools and colleges develop language curricula relevant to business. Please add an extra sheet if necessary.

2.1 Please list, in order of importance, the languages your firm's employees have used regularly and tick the skills they needed to use. Please add an extra tick for the skills you consider most important.					
Languages	Listening	Speaking	Reading	Writing	Cultural Knowledge
1					
2					
3					
4					
5					

(please add an extra sheet if required)

2.2 Please list, in order of importance, the situations (by letter) in which they have used these languages: (a) meetings, (b) travelling, (c) negotiating, (d) presentations, (e) exhibitions, (f) correspondence, (g) telephone, (h) socialising, etc. (add other situations as needed)	
Language 1	
Language 2	
Language 3	
Language 4	
Language 5	

(please add an extra sheet if required)

3.0   Your Future Foreign Language Needs

3.1 Has your firm ever encountered language barriers in business dealings?

YES [   ]   NO [   ]

If YES, which languages and in which situations (by letter- (a), (b) etc.)? [see question 2.2]	
Languages	Situations (in order of importance)
1	
2	
3	
4	
5	

3.2 To your knowledge has your firm ever lost business for lack of language skills?

YES [   ]   NO [   ]

Could you give brief examples or comments on missed chances or misunderstandings because of lack of language skills? Please add an extra sheet if necessary.

_____

_____

_____

3.3 Does your firm have plans to begin trading in any new non English speaking countries?

YES [   ]   NO [   ]

If YES, which country(ies)/regions: _____

_____

3.4 . Please indicate below which languages you believe your firm will require in the future and in which situations? : (a) meetings, (b) travelling, (c) negotiating, (d) presentations, (e) exhibitions, (f) correspondence, (g) telephone, (h) socialising, etc. (add other situations if needed)

Languages	Situations, in order of importance, in which they will be needed
1	
2	
3	
4	
5	

4.0 Cultural Barriers

4.1 Has your firm ever experienced cultural barriers in business dealings?

YES [   ]   NO [   ]

If YES, please give examples (e.g. etiquette, meetings, time etc.) Please continue on extra sheet if required.

Country(ies)	Observations/Experience

5.0 Foreign Language Training

5.1 Do you have any employees with language skills?   YES [   ]   NO [   ]

If YES, please give further details

Position	Language/Level	Observations (training, situations when required, how often used)
e.g. secretary	*Basic French*	*intensive 2 week course; handling faxes; daily*

(please add an extra sheet if required)

5.2 Has your firm undertaken language training in the last 3 years? (please tick)

YES [   ]   NO [   ]

If YES, for which languages?: _____
Comments/observations: _____
_____

continue on another sheet if necessary

5.3 Has the training improved your firm's performance?

YES [   ]   NO [   ]   DON'T KNOW [   ]

Observations: _____
_____

continue on another sheet if necessary

5.4 Do you think your firm will need language training in the next 3 years?   YES ☐   NO ☐

If YES, for which languages and skills? _____

5.5 Has your firm used any new methodology for language learning? (e.g. CD-ROMs, computer, Internet, Open-Learning or combination, etc.) _____

Is it effective?   YES ☐   NO ☐   DON'T KNOW ☐
Further comments _____

6.0   Translation

6.1 How do you handle translation <u>into</u> foreign languages for different types of documents?

Translator (please tick)	✓	Languages (eg: F, Sp, Jap.)	Type of translation (e.g. orders, sales literature, letters, faxes, technical, advertising, interpreting, etc.)
(a) professional			
(b) employee			
(c) on-line			
(d) other (please state)			

(Please continue on extra sheet if needed)

6.2 How do you handle translation <u>from</u> foreign languages for different types of documents?

Translator (please tick)	✓	Languages (eg: F, Sp, Jap,)	Type of translation(e.g. orders, sales literature, letters, faxes, technical, advertising, interpreting, etc.)
(a) professional			
(b) employee			
(c) on-line			
(d) other (please state)			

Have you any particular translation needs or problems? _____

6.3 Has your firm ever included language skills in a job advertisement.?   YES ☐   NO ☐

IF yes, please comment/give details: _____

Have you heard about the National Languages for Export Campaign?   YES ☐   NO ☐

Would you like :   Please tick

(1) information from the DTI about overcoming language barriers in trade?   ☐

(2) a summary of the findings of the survey   ☐

Thank you for your time. Completing the questionnaire is greatly appreciated because it helps us to inform European policy on languages. We would also welcome any further comments which you may wish to attach.